LUCAS BROWNE

THE STORY OF AUSTRALIA'S
LUCAS BROWNE
THE WORLD CHAMPION THAT NEVER WAS

BY GRAHAM CLARK

WITHDRAWN

hardie grant books

Published in 2017 by Hardie Grant Books, an imprint of Hardie Grant Publishing

Hardie Grant Books (Melbourne)
Building 1, 658 Church Street
Richmond, Victoria 3121
hardiegrantbooks.com.au

Hardie Grant Books (London)
5th & 6th Floors
52–54 Southwark Street
London SE1 1UN
hardiegrantbooks.co.uk

A Cataloguing-in-Publication entry is available from the catalogue of the National
Library of Australia at www.nla.gov.au

The World Champion That Never Was
ISBN 978 1 74379 331 2

Cover design by Luke Causby/Blue Cork
Typeset in Sabon by Kirby Jones
Cover image courtesy of Getty Images
Printed by McPherson's Printing Group, Maryborough, Victoria

The paper this book is printed on is certified against the
Forest Stewardship Council® Standards. FSC® promotes
environmentally responsible, socially beneficial and
economically viable management of the world's forests.

For my great mate Neil, who was always inspired by the triumph of the human spirit, by mysterious and far-flung places and by the theatre of sport. This is for you, Blox.

CONTENTS

Introduction

Once, in Grozny, there was a world title fight. I was there. I was in camp with Team 'Big Daddy' for the week leading into the clash between the vastly experienced champion, the adopted hero of Chechnya, the Uzbek Ruslan Chagaev, and Lucas Browne, only twenty-three fights into his professional career, the underdog written off by many in the Australian sporting public and many more abroad. I was in his corner that night, with the best seat in the house to view Browne's bid at sporting immortality. In that amphitheatre in Grozny, among the unrestrained fervour of the Chechen crowd, all hearts were with their champion.

The story of that fight needs to be told. It was a dramatic fight. Lucas Browne was sent to the canvas in a flurry of blows from the southpaw champion. Lesser boxers would not have risen to their feet, let alone fought back to take it up to the champ, inspired by challenging words whispered in his ear by his trainer, Rodney Williams. But beyond the drama of the battle for the title of heavyweight champion of the world, there is more that demands telling.

Lucas Browne's epic quest to gain Australian boxing's Holy Grail, a world heavyweight title, happened in Grozny. The city's decades-long history of war cast its shadow over his final preparations for the fight, but at the same time Browne was welcomed and embraced by locals in the streets and marketplaces of this unique far-flung city. The Chechen president, Ramzan Kadyrov, sponsor and friend of the champion, was a lead actor in events, having cast himself in the role of Chagaev's No. 1 supporter. That is a story in itself.

Like Grozny, Lucas 'Big Daddy' Browne is a man of contradictions. There is the imposing image of his muscular tattooed body, at odds with his articulate nature and smiling demeanour. There is the respectful, dignified side to his character; then there is the man who can be controversial and outspoken, polarising opinion. There is the divide that he creates in boxing fans – between those who believe in his ability and those who cannot see past his limitations. And there is the most unusual route he has taken to where he is today: starting out cage fighting, not having his first boxing bout until he had almost hit thirty years of age. That story needs telling, every layer of it – the story of that amazing week, the story of the city where it was staged, Grozny, the thrilling story of the fight itself, and the story of the man at the centre of it all, Lucas 'Big Daddy' Browne himself.

Why is it me telling it? Well, I was there, a part of Team 'Big Daddy' during the week in camp in Grozny preparing for the fight. I had a close-up view of all that happened. I kept a journal of the conversations, events, training schedules, official functions and drama of the whole week. Since that time in Chechnya, I have explored the stories that led up to and flowed from that week – Lucas's earlier life and career, his preparation back in Sydney's west, the tragic history of Chechnya and, of course, the subsequent drama that has thrown a pall over the events in the ring that night. I had the opportunity to write this book about Lucas Browne in Grozny, and I have taken it.

It was three years earlier that I first met the big heavyweight, when he fought Kotatsu Takehara, a Japanese heavyweight, in Brisbane, in March 2013. I was aware of the impressive stable of boxers that his manager Matt Clark, my son, was beginning to assemble. Matt invited me along that evening to have a look at this fighter with the heavy hands. Browne's record stood at fourteen fights for fourteen victories. After the first minute of the first round in Brisbane, it was fifteen fights for fifteen victories. Lucas Browne had my attention. I am a boxing fan, not a boxing expert. Like a lot of fight followers, and sports fans in general, it is the story of the underdog that inspires me most. The story of the sportsperson who, when all logic dictates they cannot possibly prevail, finds something special within and indeed does rise to the occasion – that's the story for me. They are the ones who inspire. That was Lucas Browne in Grozny. That's why his story demands to be told.

Just after the fight, as we all sat together in the change room deep below Grozny's Colosseum Sports Hall, barely capable of processing what had just transpired, little did we know that the story had only just begun. Lucas Browne's battle in the ring came down to skill, self-belief and courage;

his battle outside it had more to do with notions of honesty, character and judgement.

In the months that were to follow, the boxer would be embroiled in not one, but two drug controversies, putting at risk everything he had fought for. Everything was plunged into a darkness from which we have not emerged.

I was there in Grozny when one battle was fought and won, and the first silent shots in the other had already been fired. Let me take you there.

CHAPTER ONE

The Chill of Moscow

I. Grozny Chronicle – Saturday, 27 February 2016

Lucas 'Big Daddy' Browne will fight the champion Ruslan 'White Tyson' Chagaev for the World Boxing Association regular world heavyweight title in Grozny, Chechnya. Chagaev is the rumbling, skilled craftsman of the ring, an awkward southpaw with a thick neck and a stubborn head that defies being knocked out. Lucas Browne is the power puncher with heavy hands and the heart of a lion. Now he has something new: mentor, friend and trainer Rodney Williams. With the opportunity of a shot at the world title, Lucas has a more intense focus on fitness, foot movement and the fundamentals of defence. Together, through sheer willpower made manifest in endless hours of drills, they have taken this wild wrecking-ball warrior with the powerful V8 engine and tuned it up, modifying it, adding a level of finesse to the brute muscle power. The word out of Grozny is that the machine is humming.

Browne and Williams have been in camp in Grozny for three days. With them is Philippe Fondu, a key member of the support team, an influential negotiator and matchmaker who helped put this opportunity together. He is also one of the finest cornermen in boxing. Tomorrow, Lucas's manager, Matt Clark, will join them, as will I. On Wednesday, Lucas's older brother, Danny, younger brother, Pat, and friend and sponsor Matt Meyerhoff will complete the small band of true believers in Grozny.

Grozny – the city that for decades Australians have been advised to avoid, the hive in which swarmed Chechen rebels, which spawned Islamic extremists, which harboured the notorious Russian mafia, a place of war and lawlessness, the Badlands. Will the reality match the reputation? We will all travel there with some degree of apprehension, convinced that the deck will be stacked against Lucas Browne. He dares to challenge the champion in his heartland. You can't help but imagine the gathering crowd will be hostile, siding with their hero, baying for the blood of the intruder.

For the moment Matt and I are in the President's Hotel in Moscow, from which we look out towards the Kremlin, St Basil's Cathedral and Red Square, centuries of living history right before our eyes. A demonstration is underway. Here, one year ago, opposition figurehead and open Putin critic Boris Nemtsov was assassinated as he walked across the Bolshoy Moskvoretsky Bridge, which spans the Moscow River alongside the Kremlin. The assassin's bullets pierced Nemtsov's vital organs; the sounds of the shots reverberated against the Kremlin walls and all around the world. As we try to make our way through the chaos, a tall Russian senses our confusion and offers to navigate us through the crowds and police barricades over to Red Square. He confidently strides through a spider web of subways and checkpoints guarded by armed police, glancing back over his shoulder, making sure that we are following. In a circumspect tone, he whispers that the cold-blooded killing was the work of Chechen gunmen. A sense of foreboding descends. Indeed, two Chechens have been arrested for the killing; one suspect has blown himself up in his Grozny apartment. We do not tell our Russian guide where we are going tomorrow.

Now the mood is wintry and austere as we look upon Lenin's Tomb in Red Square. Soldiers dressed in great coats, fur lining the collars, stare blankly ahead, teeth clenched against the cold. St Basil's Cathedral seems at odds with its surroundings, its green-and-yellow-, blue-and-white domes vivid against the grey sky, like the last flower defying a blanket of frost.

The sun sets, a bitter cold descends and an icy wind is upon us. Nature hisses. Hunched over against the cold, snow flurries hurling themselves into our downcast faces, we retrace our journey to the President's Hotel, back in through the guarded boom gates, into the relieving warmth of the hotel foyer. When in Moscow, do as the Muscovites do, so we seat ourselves at the opulent marble bar and order vodka, neat.

Matt pulls out his mobile and presses Lucas's number. We learn that all is on track in Grozny. With a week to go, he has no nagging injuries. He's as fit as he has ever been for a fight and his training routine is now all about maintaining focus and sharpness, having him primed for the night. He seems very upbeat.

As Matt and I settle comfortably on the barstools, our conversation is all about the opportunity that has been *presented to Browne. Matt has been his manager since just before he defeated Colin Wilson to win the Australian title in the eleventh fight of his professional career, four years ago now. We talk of fights since and fights that could lie ahead in the future – the WBA has a complicated system, and has a tournament drawn up for a series of bouts to clarify things. No one expects Browne to be part of it after this bout with Chagaev. But if he wins he will be the WBA regular heavyweight champion of the world. The WBA has an unusual category on top of that – but only sometimes. It recognises the other boxing organisations – the WBC, the WBO and the IBF – and if a boxer holds two of their three titles, the WBA designates him its super champion. At the moment, the British fighter Tyson Fury is the WBA super champion. The WBA plans to have its regular champ fight Fury or whoever defeats him. We know the boxing world does not expect Lucas Browne to proceed past this fight in Grozny, but we dare to believe.*

We don't doubt that the examination that lies ahead in the ring in Grozny will be anything other than torrid. But Lucas Browne will not die wondering and if this fight comes down to a test of fortitude, he will pass. As we walk over to the lifts to our rooms, Matt recalls a similar challenge that Lucas faced, one that he overcame in spectacular fashion.

II. A Test of Fortitude

Early in 2015, the World Boxing Association moved Lucas Browne up its rankings to become its No. 2 heavyweight in the world, making him the mandatory challenger to its reigning regular world champion, Ruslan Chagaev. In the minds of many boxing fans and experts, in Australia and throughout the world, Browne had already outperformed his potential and was a challenger for a world title in name only. On the positive side, there was no doubting that Browne had enormous power, a granite chin and a proud spirit.

Some argued that these very strengths masked Browne's deficiencies as a top-level boxer. They argued that he knocked out lesser opponents before they could expose his weaknesses. According to his critics, the weaknesses included a deficient defence, a lack of evasiveness, a heaviness of foot and a limited kitbag of combination punches.

In their eyes Browne lacked the ringcraft that a boxer needed to succeed at the highest level. He had not had a grounding in amateur ranks, where a boxer learns his trade, graduating from a raw apprentice to a skilled tradesman. But here he was, standing at the door of Ruslan Chagaev's world title. The WBA had just opened the door for him. Whether he could force his way in and take Chagaev's crown was the question. Browne was not an individual to get ahead of himself. He knew better than anyone that he was on a steep learning curve. But he also knew the arsenal that he had at his disposal: the ability to wear a big shot and respond with arguably the heaviest right hand in world heavyweight boxing. His ability had delivered much success to him already. By the time he was to face Chagaev, his record of twenty-three bouts, twenty-three victories, twenty of them by knockout, spoke for itself. And one of those knockout victories, in April 2014, saw Browne become Australia's first Commonwealth heavyweight champion since Peter Jackson defeated the Englishman Jem Smith in 1886. That fight, for a title that had some history and substance to it, was his biggest test of character to that point.

He had travelled to the industrial Yorkshire city of Sheffield about a week before his showdown with the Canadian Eric Martel Bahoeli for the then vacant title. Bahoeli, nicknamed 'The Hammer', had disposed of his three previous opponents by knockout – and came to Sheffield expecting a similar result. Browne had done some homework on his opponent, watching his fights on YouTube, and he knew that the former ice hockey player was an athletic and awkward target. Browne went into the bout very confident that he could land some of his heavy hits, which would eventually take their toll.

Supporting him in Sheffield that evening were his then trainer Tama Te Huna, manager Matt Clark and experienced cornerman Philippe Fondu.

Not for the first time, Browne went into the fight feeling very relaxed and in control, but, as a result, started slowly and a bit off the pace. As he puts it, with unguarded candour: 'A lot of the time I have to be punched once or twice to wake up and get into the fight.'

In that first round he did indeed get punched a couple of times. Bahoeli outjabbed him with his quick hands, and managed to rock the Australian with one or two heavier shots. Browne was finding Bahoeli a difficult target, but started to find his range in the second, landing a huge overhand right flush on his opponent's upper jaw. Bahoeli slumped to the canvas, but at the count of eight he staggered to his feet and the referee signalled the boxers to fight on. Browne sensed blood in the water and pursued his prey around the ring, but

Bahoeli kept moving and avoided further heavy damage until the bell sounded.

In the third round the fight completely changed. With both fighters wanting to snatch the advantage, they rushed each other, heads bobbing in defence. Browne ducked down to the left just as Martel Bahoeli came in from the right, his forehead collecting Browne right on the stretched skin over his left eyebrow, opening a gaping cut that flopped down over his eye. The referee had the ringside doctor inspect the ugly wound, but he deemed that the fight could continue. Suddenly the fight was in the balance and Bahoeli went after the big Australian, targeting the deep gash in an attempt to finish proceedings then and there.

As cuts man Fondu worked on the gash during the break, Clark told his fighter what he needed to hear: 'The cut's fine, it's nothing to worry about.'

So Browne answered the bell for the start of round four, confident that all was still on track. Most of that confidence was washed away, however, when the referee again paused proceedings, with a minute to go in the round, for the doctor to take another look at the wound. Again he nodded fight on, but not before he informed the Australian that if the cut deteriorated further, he would be stopping the fight at the end of the round.

Suddenly, there were deep concerns in his camp and in his own mind that the fight could be snatched away from him due to the accidental head clash. So he took things into his own hands. For the rest of that fourth round he was the hunter, cornering Bahoeli and letting fly with numerous rights, seeking a way through for the killer blow. But the bell rang and 'Big Daddy' was breathing heavily in his corner. The referee was prepared to let the fight enter the fifth round.

Browne had more to give and was determined to put this fight to bed. In the fifth round he zeroed in on his target. He manoeuvred Bahoeli onto the ropes and again went to work with his clubbing right hand, one of which sneaked through his opponent's defences and found its target, coming down around Bahoeli's left ear. The fight was all but over at that point. Bahoeli still somehow stayed on his feet, under a barrage of rights, and then was clipped by an unexpected left hand. Browne had set him up for a wicked right uppercut that drew the curtains on his opponent's night out. Browne stood, arms raised in triumph, his corner ecstatic in celebration, their man the new Commonwealth heavyweight champion.

It would have been easy at that point to get swept away on a wave of optimism and euphoria and claim readiness for the likes of the Ukrainian Wladimir Klitschko, who has been the preeminent heavyweight fighter of the twenty-first century. But in a post-fight interview Browne demonstrated his inner self-control and moderating self-assessment when he declared he was not yet ready to take on that standard of fighter. He was aware of his own technical limitations.

Browne knew at that point that he lacked the polish and ringcraft to match it with a champion of that elite standard. Equally, Browne knew he possessed a tremendous right hand and the burning desire to improve. Deep within, he believed that he would be ready one day – but was not ready yet.

Further, Browne said of his Commonwealth title victory:

I don't want to cheapen that title for anyone, but it
doesn't really mean much to me at all. For me it still
means most people don't know who I am. In my mind
it was always going to be a stepping stone to bigger and
better things and that is a world title in the end.

That was the Lucas Browne of 2014, Commonwealth
heavyweight champion, delivering on his potential, delighting
his horde of fans – and keeping one eye on the future. Fast-
forward to March 2016 and much had changed. By the
time Browne had been installed as mandatory challenger to
Chagaev, he had scored three further victories in the ring. The
most recent of them was against the American Julius Long,
who, at 216 centimetres, or 7 foot 1 in imperial measure, was
an awkward, towering opponent who stretched Browne, a
difficult customer to put away. But dispatch him Browne did
with a victory in the ninth round. The pathway to Ruslan
Chagaev and a world title now lay ahead.

In the meantime the world champion had contracted to
fight fellow southpaw Francesco Pianeta and Browne's camp
accepted a step-aside fee to permit that fight to proceed in
Germany. Chagaev was untroubled, scoring a knockout win
in the first round against the Italian. So now the world WBA
champion looked towards his Australian challenger, and
surely must have thought another swift victory lay ahead.
The venue and terms of the fight were settled: Chagaev versus
Browne, Saturday 5 March 2016, at the Colosseum Sports
Hall in Grozny, Chechnya.

Grozny, a city with so many stories to tell, most of them horror stories. Grozny, a city that lives somewhere in the Western subconscious, though most have never seen it. Grozny, a place name associated with war and the worst of human behaviour. But now Lucas Browne and his entourage would travel there in an attempt to raid the king's treasure. What would they find?

Maybe a city whose visage had been disfigured, acid thrown in her face, her features dissolved, her beauty stolen. Who assaulted Grozny? Who threw the acid? Well, there's a story to tell there, but to tell it we need to go a little back in time, well before an Australian heavyweight ventured to its door, back to a time when another heavyweight reigned supreme.

CHAPTER TWO

So This Is Grozny

I. Grozny Chronicle – Sunday, 28 February 2016

*A newly fallen blanket of pristine snow masks the sombre
bland landscape that sprawls out from the highway leading
from the heart of Moscow to Domodedovo Airport. We check
in for our Red Wings flight to Grozny and a bus transports
us, along with about a hundred other passengers, across the
tarmac to our flight. Most of our fellow passengers are young
men, coincidentally boxers themselves returning home from
a tournament in Moscow. They joke and laugh among each
other in the way of young men, a way that transcends place
and culture. Many wear T-shirts with some variation of the
same basic message, 'Defend Grozny', coupled with the
silhouette of an AK-47 assault rifle. There's an irony there:
the AK-47 is the same gun known as the Kalashnikov, named
after its designer, Mikhail Kalashnikov, a Russian.*

*We leave Moscow below us at 12.15 pm as we fly south
towards the Chechen capital. Chechnya is landlocked
by Russia proper to its north and Georgia to its south,
sandwiched east and west by the lesser known republics*

of Dagestan and Ingushetia. The geography of this part of the world is dominated by great seas and mountains: the Black Sea to the west, the Caspian Sea to the east and the Caucasus Mountain Range sprawling between them, taking in Europe's highest peak, the majestic Mount Elbrus. The landscapes are breathtaking, but it is the history that intrigues me. Chechnya is a region laid waste, flattened from without and then festering from within. And now, we are told, back on its feet; we shall soon see for ourselves, as two hours have passed and we have touched down.

A large banner is draped across the wall of the arrivals lounge, in English and Chechen: 'Welcome to Chechen Republic'. Even something as simple as that message contains history and politics: Chechen has variously been written in the Arabic, Latin and Cyrillic (Russian) scripts. In 1992, as it declared independence from Russia, it reverted from Cyrillic to Latin; after Russia won the war, Cyrillic was reimposed. As I contemplated my surroundings, a young man with our hotel logo emblazoned on his shirt greets us and leads us to his car. We are now in Grozny, that place of grim tales and human suffering, the ground zero of the decades-long Russian–Chechen conflict, the most completely destroyed city in history, where not a single building was left undamaged by war.

This then is the city that the Russians decreed should no longer stand, a city to be razed. What of the misery for the civilian population? What must it have been like? Again, a clue lies in the language. 'Grozny' means 'terrible.' It is the same word as in 'Ivan the Terrible', the fourteenth-century tsar who conquered Siberia, the 'first tsar of all the Russians', as he is known. Even then, there is a double meaning: in modern English 'terrible' is better translated as 'fearsome' – and indeed, the Russians fear the Chechens, particularly those from Grozny.

But we have not arrived into a neglected, desolate wasteland of still-smouldering ruins. They have been busy rebuilding, for we drive into the city through neat housing projects, neighbourhood blocks, shops and businesses and great mosques. Lucas Browne and Ruslan Chagaev stare out at us from billboards and banners. For this week only, images of the President of the Chechen Republic, Ramzan Kadyrov, and his deceased father, the much revered Akhmad Kadyrov, compete with those of the boxers. And also with images of Michael Buffer, the American ring announcer whose trademark catchphrase 'Let's get ready to rumble!' will be the spark that ignites the fire in the Colosseum Sports Hall.

I look from my car window upon shoppers walking the footpaths, some with children by their sides, some looking down at their mobile phones as they go about their business. The ordinariness of what I see is simultaneously comforting and disorientating. I expected a city still in chaos, pockmarked by violence, its people slinking around, cowed and threatened. I have not been transported to a Caucasian Mogadishu or a besieged and bleeding Aleppo, but instead to a functioning, apparently stable, modern metropolis.

All my preconceptions are now challenged when our driver swerves around a corner and I catch my first glimpse of ultra-modern skyscrapers – Las Vegas or Surfers Paradise in downtown Grozny. They stand towering over the rest of the city, like proud citadels from which any defender could scan the far horizons for the approach of invaders. But when we arrive at that nest of buildings, we find their function is as Western and modern as their design; the buildings are office spaces, gyms and hotels. Indeed, one of the tallest of them is the Grozny City Hotel, our accommodation while in camp as Lucas prepares for his world title shot.

As much as appearances say otherwise, it is not some Western tourist strip in which we have arrived; it is Grozny. The hotel, along with the other six buildings that stand by its side, are an enclosed compound, protected by boom gates manned by guards with heavy assault weapons. As our car pulls up at the gates, one of the guards nonchalantly glances at us and the boom gates rise. The disconnection between armed security and the luxury now before me makes my head spin.

Grozny City Hotel is an architectural landmark, a streamlined towering symbol of Grozny's rebirth. One of seven similar buildings in the complex, its five-star foyer is adorned with replica world title belts, life-size Styrofoam images of all the combatants on the card and, of course, most prominent of all are those of Lucas Browne and Ruslan Chagaev.

But before we can enter the lobby, we pass into an airlock between two doors, an outer and an inner door separated by only a metre or two in a narrow entrance which, in turn, permits access to a vestibule. Here sit two armed security staff, weapons holstered, faces vigilant, and from there we step onto the platform of the huge revolving door that delivers us to the hotel foyer.

Matt and I check in with the young receptionist, who looks as stylish as the staff of any fashionable hotel in Rome or

Paris. She sits behind a long marble counter and speaks fluent English. She provides our room cards and we learn that floor twenty-four is headquarters for Team 'Big Daddy'. We learn the configuration: each floor has the lifts and service wells centred, surrounded by a square-shaped hallway, with the ten rooms opening outwards. We exit the lift to a silent floor.

Lucas hears our arrival and steps out of his room to greet us. Standing before me is the big man, his 195-centimetre frame – 6 foot 5 – looking chiselled and fit. The sheer size of the man, combined with the rippling muscles and the startling tattoos, guarantees he dominates any room. But it's not just that. His piercing blue eyes give a hint of the intriguing character and high intellect that lie within. When he speaks, the voice is more that of an artist or actor than a fighter. Trainer Rodney Williams joins us.

Team 'Big Daddy' has started to take shape. We are welcomed enthusiastically and, in some surreal way, we feel like we have arrived at a bunkered-down fortress, deep in the wild lands, arriving like reinforcements at a siege. This is not as far-fetched as it sounds, for we have travelled to this most perilous of places, far from the familiar and comfortable, delivering support to this boxer who aspires to achieve what none of his countrymen have ever achieved. The handshakes and greetings are warm and sincere. The team has just grown by two and this seems to have buoyed Lucas.

The big man is in fine spirits, but he is looking for the interaction that some new arrivals can provide. Lucas is in room 2309, where we sit. He tells us about the warmth of his Chechen welcome; in Grozny, Lucas is a rock star. He talks about his fitness: the bathroom scales in his room tell him he is down to 115 kilograms, light by his standards. We discuss his improved footwork, agility and head movement, his strengthened left rip to accompany his lethal right. We talk about his head space, how he's feeling.

And we cannot help but talk tactics. There is little doubt that the champion will try to assert himself early in the fight by coming at him. Lucas has options; in his words, a bit of Ali and a bit of Foreman, meaning that he hopes to have the foot movement to back-pedal when needed. He knows he has the firepower to launch his own heavy assaults when the opportunity presents.

I have watched his progress over the past few months in heavy training and, speaking to him now, I believe that he may well have undergone some fundamental metamorphosis in his style under Rodney's tutelage; never before would anyone, certainly not Lucas himself, have talked about his style and that of the man who could 'float like a butterfly and sting like a bee' in the same breath. Not for a moment is the man comparing himself to the legendary Muhammad Ali; he makes the point that he has always been able to hit like George Foreman, but now he has agility and fitness to accompany the power.

The looming world title fight is all we want to talk about. Matt shares his thoughts about the importance of giving Chagaev something to think about in the initial rounds, maybe a snapping jab as he comes in on the prowl, or, if he leaves himself open after throwing one of his trademark lefts, a return right rip to his unprotected ribs. Lucas knows it, but his thinking at this stage is not to take unnecessary risks early in the fight. He says he'd be happy to win it in the twelfth if that's how it pans out. Patience is a valuable commodity when fighting a cagey veteran like Chagaev and many a challenger in the history of boxing has been cut down by his own rush of blood. Control will be the key. Rodney will be happy for Lucas to feel his way into the fight; foot and head movement will be a priority, avoiding early carnage, and then, when an opportunity presents – strike like a cobra.

Lucas's self-talk is all positive. His thumb knuckle on his huge right hand, broken in the recent bout against the appropriately named Richard Towers, is giving no reason for concern. The word is that Chagaev can't see well from a permanently damaged left eye and Lucas intends to close the right with one of his head-jolting jabs. He believes.

Reality reaches out and snatches my attention. Three Chechen bodyguards are in the background, one sitting in a lounge chair, two standing, but all observing. Any complacency I may have already developed about the cauldron we find ourselves in has just been swept away.

Two teams of three guards have been assigned to protect the fighter. Sitting outside my room affords them the best view to his room, the lifts and the service-well area. They speak no English, but confident professionalism speaks its own language.

They are all young men, with a swagger about them, and no doubt are highly trained. Their assignment is to keep Lucas alive for the fight. The challenger being assassinated in his hotel room by militants or extremists would not serve the reputation of Chechnya well. They have been assigned this task directly from the office of President Kadyrov; the world is watching.

Lucas and Rodney have been taking all their meals in the restaurant atop our building, but they have learned of a local pizzeria that they want to try for dinner this evening. Rather than its reputation for fine food, its name is what has attracted their attention: Hal Al Pacino's. So, on our very first night in Grozny, Matt and I do what all the travel and government agencies advised us not to do; we venture out from the safety of our compound.

Our team has been assigned some other staff, less confronting than our armed guards. Ruslan will be our driver, at our disposal whenever he is required. The quiet nature and humble smile of this middle-aged Chechen fills the void created by the absence of a shared language. Here to help in that regard is Ibrahim, one of our two assigned translators, the other being Adam, who completed his first shift of three days shortly before Matt and I arrived. They are both young men, university educated, refined and cultured. Their task will be vital, not just in the mundane duties of interpreting menus and the like, but when the business end of the week arrives. Language cannot be a barrier to information.

So Ruslan performs his duty and deposits us at Hal Al Pacino's, a mere five-minute drive from our guarded precinct but way out there in unchartered seas. We step onto the cement footpath and look upon the restaurant, so similar to any small Italian eatery at home. We haven't made a booking but, this being a Sunday evening, there is only one couple dining, with about seven or eight tables vacant. The five of us – Lucas, Rodney, Matt, myself and Ibrahim – sit together at one of those tables while a metre or two away sit our posse of vigilant guards. Tonight, Ibby, as he has immediately become known, has translation duties, and we order and enjoy pizzas that are no different to those back home.

Other customers come and go, seemingly for takeaway orders, and some start to recognise the big man sitting quietly in the corner of the room. It seems a citizen of Grozny would have to have been living under a rock of late not to recognise the challenger, so numerous are the billboards and advertisements festooning the city. Recognise him they do and, during the evening, quite a few pluck up the courage to request – and be granted – a photograph. Lucas is ever sociable and obliging, making many a Chechen's night this evening.

Our dinner is done and we approach our hostess who is stationed behind the counter at her cash register. Lucas has the local currency of Russian roubles and approaches the counter to pay the bill. Having politely stayed in the background going about her business all evening, the lady is not going to let this moment pass her by and she, like her Chechen customers before her, requests a photo with the huge Australian.

Lucas is reminded just how far we are from home when he motions to put his arm around her shoulders – and the woman steps away defensively. Of course we are in a deeply religious Islamic place, where it is a big no-no to touch a woman in public. With an apology given, the lady stands slightly removed from Lucas and the photo is taken. It is just a little reminder to us all of the importance of paying heed to social and cultural norms. Back in our hotel on the twenty-fourth floor, it is now 10 pm and the four of us stand outside Rodney's room. Our conversation is drawn inexorably back to the epicentre of our personal cyclone, the showdown on Saturday night. Matt notes that it is a huge undercard with twelve fights leading up to the title bout, meaning that Lucas could be in for a long evening, even before he steps into the ring. Rodney is timing Lucas's workouts later at night to tune his body rhythms for a late-night fight. Details like that can make all the difference. Matt adds that many of the earlier fights, which all involve boxers from the local Akhmat Fight Club, are likely to finish early. Good point: the night might speed past more quickly than we anticipate. It is a variable that will be hard to pin down.

Rodney suggests that, later in the week, he needs to sit down with Matt and determine exactly how our corner will function on Saturday night; another fine detail that must be ticked off.

All this time, as we four Australians drawl on, the four Chechens stand a few metres away in the hallway, talking quietly among themselves, the guards sounding and appearing relaxed and light-hearted. If it is at all possible to be casual and professionally vigilant at the very same time, this is how these men seem to me. Perhaps it is my inability to seriously accept the possibility of imminent danger to Lucas and to us. Could there really be an assassination attempt on the life of a world title contender?

Well, that gets back to where we are and what is at stake for others. Perhaps there can be more at stake than my myopic view suggests, more than a mere title belt. Maybe here in Grozny, for some, this could represent an opportunity to draw attention to a cause, to strike down what your enemy builds and to destroy what he cherishes.

Chechnya, technically, is not Chechnya; it is the Chechen Republic, part of the Russian Federation. It is a nation, but not a nation. Its currency is the Russian rouble. A domestic Red Wings flight delivered us from Moscow to Grozny with no passport required. It is autonomous, but not independent. It has its own president, Ramzan Kadyrov, who will loom large in the story of Lucas Browne. Son of the assassinated Chechen leader Akhmad Kadyrov, installed as president in 2007, Ramzan Kadyrov is widely seen as a keen supporter of Russian president Vladimir Putin.

President Akhmad Kadyrov was once a leader in the armed resistance to the Russian forces in support of Chechen independence. In the second Chechen war starting in 1999 he switched sides, and now, with Russian backing, his son Ramzan has brought a sense of calm and stability to a place rocked by war and civil strife, exercising control over the Republic with a firm and, at times, intimidating presence.

What I can see clearly is that, out of the rubble of destruction, Kadyrov's presidency has rebuilt this city and imposed civil order; Grozny now has a vibrant beating heart. I stand surrounded by first-world luxury but only a few metres from a loaded handgun, yet strangely I not only feel safe, but exhilarated. I am where I want to be, in a party preparing for a heavyweight title fight, in a place that contradicts a lot of what I have grown to take for granted – and I am feeling pumped. What sports fan wouldn't be?

Our language and cultural barriers are beginning to crumble. We learn that our three guards are named Shamil, Abubakar and Aslan. I am reminded of Aslan the lion in C. S. Lewis's The Chronicles of Narnia, *a name the author* took up as it is a name in this part of the world that means 'lion'. And it suits our bodyguard: he boasts the biggest physique of his colleagues, and looks like a rugby league forward. At about 190 centimetres and a very fit-looking 105 kilograms, he has the sort of body to intimidate and destroy those who would challenge him. But he has the demeanour and manners of a polite, respectful schoolboy. Via Ibby's translation, Aslan approaches Rodney and asks him for advice about boxing technique.

It reminds me that these men are fighters of a different sort, but fighters all the same, and they must have the assignment of their lives, being part of the preparation for a world title fight. Rodney doesn't hesitate and dons the hit-pads. Our Chechen protector, dressed in jeans and a light jumper, has the gloves on and is thumping the pads with force. He has power and looks formidable. Rodney circles him, weaving his hands out in front of his own face, presenting moving targets for the Chechen to aim at. As he does so, he talks, through Ibby's translation, about weight transference and swivelling the hips as a punch is delivered. He looks at Aslan's feet, advising that everything starts there. The big man has a very square stance with his feet spread apart, not allowing for fluent movement, limiting his reach. Ibrahim's Chechen interpretation of Rodney's instructions results in Aslan adjusting his stance, straightening up his feet. The man is a quick learner and is now punching with more rhythm and timing.

Rodney now stands in the hallway facing the bodyguard, who listens intently to the translation, gloved fists by his side. Rod explains to him that there are three distances in boxing – thinking-space distance where you can't be hit, *straight-punch distance where you are close enough to land and receive a jab, but nothing more, and finally looping-punch distance, where round-arm blows are possible. The big Chechen stands, eyes intently on Rodney, absorbing everything he is saying.*

I have two thoughts. This man has been trained in self-defence and could probably kill in myriad ways, but, with less than an hour of Rodney's tuition, he suddenly looks like a boxer. If he so chose, he could grow to be quite a fighter in the ring.

My second thought is what a wonderful teacher Rodney is. He focuses on fundamental skills, simplifies them and presents them in such a way that his pupil is gently extended further and further. And, like the finest of teachers, he can connect with the heart just as much as the mind. He seems to be a mentor with a gentle patience and an almost innate awareness of human character. He has that knack of making people feel special. In the manner of all his fellow countrymen thus far, Aslan humbly thanks us, shaking the hands of each of us. If anyone was to attack us, Aslan could now outbox them – although I'm not sure that would be his (or our) first preference. In Matt's room, three of us close this first night together in Grozny with a whisky. Not Ibby, as he is a devout Muslim, and not Lucas – he does not drink. He has seen too much alcohol-fuelled violence as a bouncer; drinking holds no attraction. I sit at my desk in the early hours concluding my journal for our first day here in Chechnya. I think about this exotic place in which I find myself, where the challenge of his life awaits Lucas Browne. My journal concludes with a question that has troubled me ever since Grozny presented itself as the venue for his shot at the world title. As I look around me at the luxury of this ultra-modern hotel room, I wonder what events could have possibly led to the obliteration of a once beautiful city.

II. Who Threw the Acid?

As Adolf Hitler rose to become German Chancellor in 1933, he had a doctrine to sell to his people, one that would unify those who were willing to buy it, galvanising them and steeling them for what was to come. The ideology that he preached proclaimed their ethnic superiority; those of the Aryan race were the 'chosen ones'. He spat out this gospel of hatred, convincing a nation seeking simple solutions to its problems that they were indeed a master race. In six years' time he would lead them to war on that lie. But before war, the dictator used a different theatre in which to demonstrate ethnic superiority: sport. Planned as the event that would showcase the Nazi dogma of racial superiority to the world, the Berlin Olympic Games became instead a stage for Jesse Owens, the inspirational African-American athlete, who returned home with four track-and-field gold medals, winning the 100 and 200 metres, the long jump and his share of the American 4 x 100 metre relay. Jesse Owens had crashed that party. Perhaps the Nazi creed would be more successfully demonstrated in the boxing ring?

On 22 June 1938, Max Schmeling stepped into the ring in Yankee Stadium in the Bronx, New York, to fight Joe Louis. More rode on the result than the world heavyweight title. They had met two years before in the same venue and the former world champion Schmeling had handed the number one contender Louis his first defeat, knocking him out in the twelfth round. Now, with war drums beating in Europe, the current world champion had been summoned to the White House and informed by President Franklin D. Roosevelt that American morale needed a Joe Louis victory.

Schmeling had been accompanied to New York by a Nazi entourage, one of whom declared that a German could not be beaten by a man of Joe Louis's race. Schmeling had become the propaganda tool of the fascist regime, very much against his wishes.

In fact, Schmeling displayed remarkable courage at times in defying the wishes of his government, and even those of the Fuhrer himself. Despite pressure from the highest levels of the Nazi Party, Schmeling maintained a professional relationship with his Jewish promoter, Joe Jacobs. Schmeling reportedly saved the lives of several Jewish children in Berlin during the Nazi persecution of the race, secreting them in his apartment, at serious personal risk. But in June 1938, he had one purpose only: to regain the world heavyweight title.

Back then, the Louis–Schmeling fight was the biggest show on earth. Joe Louis was cast in the role of the humble, polite African-American, the one-time poor man from the land of opportunity. And, of course, Max Schmeling represented aggression and hatred, almost a microcosm of all the evil of Nazi Germany. Totally inaccurately and unfairly for the German fighter, the fight was reduced to 'Joe Democracy versus Max Fascist'.

However, it is not stretching the point too far to contend that Roosevelt was right and the world did indeed need a Joe

Louis victory. The vitriol spilled over on the fight night, with the German entering the ring beneath a shower of rubbish thrown by the crowd. It was all over in the first round.

Louis attacked his opponent from the outset, throwing a whirlwind of punches and forcing the German back against the ropes. Schmeling went down to the canvas three times in the first two minutes. The referee stopped the fight. Joe Louis had retained his heavyweight world title in what had perhaps been the most high-profile battle of the century. Battles of a more tragic and monumental scale were not far away.

Less than fourteen months later, Germany would launch blitzkrieg upon Poland and World War II had commenced. Both boxers found themselves with a new purpose and role. With the outbreak of war, Louis enlisted in the United States army and was designated duties where his celebrity could support troop morale and generally boost the American war effort. On the other hand, Schmeling was ostracised by the Nazis after his loss to Louis and was drafted into the Luftwaffe, seeing combat as a paratrooper. He was discharged when deemed medically unfit after sustaining a gunshot wound to his knee during the battle for Crete in 1941, fighting against Australians.

By the second half of 1943, Schmeling had recovered from his injuries. The fighting on the Eastern Front had enveloped much of the Soviet Union and focused on the Caucasus region, an area rich in the prized commodity, that necessity for war, oil. With it, the German advance could continue. Without it, the German thrust would be halted, its machines of destruction silenced. So now, oil-producing states such as Chechnya became strategically important, not to mention even more productive oil fields beyond Chechnya. Joseph Stalin was every bit as evil as Hitler. Devoid of human empathy, the Russian leader could be just as ruthless as the German dictator. Stalin was unsettled by the Chechen uprising in the early 1940s, and suspected that Chechen leaders were negotiating with German officials behind his back. There is only speculation as to the degree of collaboration that took place, but, as Stalin saw it, the Germans wanted oil and the Chechens wanted independence from Russia. So he took matters into his own hands. In February 1944, genocide commenced in Chechnya. The entire Chechen population – up to half a million people – was to be expelled, loaded like livestock onto railway carriages and deported to Soviet satellite countries such as Kazakhstan. Those that weren't deported were slaughtered, shot or burned alive in their villages. Many of those who were deported died of exposure or starvation along the way. An entire population was dispossessed of their land, torn from their ancestral home. While in exile, their homes were bestowed on the Russians made homeless by the German armies, thus completing the pillaging of a proud people. The Chechens' past was erased, their books burned, their gravestones destroyed, their language banned. Their placenames were changed, their mosques flattened. It was as if these people had never existed, their tomorrow snatched from them, their today obliterated, their yesterday wiped clean. Chechnya was now Russian, in rule, in language and in people.

One of the many to be deported – and one who survived – was a man by the name of Hamid Saidov. He has a role to play in the story of Lucas Browne, which we will come to.

May 1945 brought an end to the war in Europe. Hitler was dead, his armies vanquished. But it would be another eight years until the other megalomaniacal tyrant, Joseph Stalin, would pass away in 1953, dead of a stroke that felled him at his dacha outside Moscow. The Chechen people were still in exile, their land still occupied. It would be another four long years before the Soviets would pass laws protecting and restoring some rights to repressed peoples and nations within their borders. As a result, Chechens were permitted to return to their homeland after more than a decade in exile.

The Russians directed their return to their homeland away from the more isolated mountainous regions towards Grozny, city centres where the Chechens could be more readily integrated among the occupying peoples, diluting their zeal for independence and homogenising their ethnic spirit.

Finding their homes in the possession of relocated Russians, Belarusians, Ukrainians and Dagestanis, the Chechens were understandably resentful and quickly became the marginalised and underprivileged of the new society. Management and government roles went to Russian speakers; low-skilled and lowly paid positions went to Chechens.

How could a Chechen hope to secure a good job when the schools did not teach in the Chechen language? It wouldn't be until the final decade of the twentieth century that the Chechens would again be taught in their own language. Disadvantage proved a fertile breeding ground for crime, violence and discontent. And, as the twentieth century grew older, and the Soviet state crumbled, the desire to shake off the yoke of Russian rule reawakened. Chechen independence again became a force to be reckoned with.

Then, by 1994, Russian president Boris Yeltsin had had enough of the Chechen rumblings. He instructed his military to deal with the matter. The first Chechen war was about to be launched, very soon followed by the second, conflicts that would see the total devastation of Grozny. The aerial bombing would be the acid rain in the face of Grozny. Hamid Saidov was condemned to watch history repeat itself, as the Chechens again had to withstand the Russians.

Lucas Browne was a fifteen-year-old schoolboy living on the other side of the world, in Sydney's western suburbs, finding his own strength, completely oblivious to the storm about to descend on Grozny.

CHAPTER THREE

Becoming 'Big Daddy'

I. Grozny Chronicle – Monday, 29 February 2016

I have been woken early, just after 5 am I think, by the call to prayer from the mosque that sits just below our hotel. We learn later that it is the Akhmad Kadyrov Mosque, known to locals as the 'Heart of Chechnya'. It was commissioned by President Kadyrov and named in honour of his father. Completed in 2008, the mosque, with its stunning design and breathtaking spires, holds pride of place on the huge city centre block that is the Islamic Complex. In the fresh air of the dawning day, the muezzin's voice, amplified through a loudspeaker, carries clearly up to our twenty-fourth floor. The faithful are being called to prayer and it reminds me that we are in a deeply devout Muslim nation. I start my day.

The buffet breakfast is provided on the third floor of the hotel and the four of us catch the lift down together. Lucas has slept well and, this morning, a day closer to his title showdown, he is as relaxed as ever. Continental and cooked breakfasts are available. Lucas has a big motor to run and tucks into the eggs that the chef fries in the open kitchen and slides straight onto his plate.

We sit together at a small table, sharing the cafeteria with about twenty other guests. I indulge in my drug of choice, caffeine, just as Philippe Fondu approaches our table. Philippe is a vastly experienced, multiskilled boxing negotiator and businessman, central to the brokered deal that has brought Lucas to Chechnya. He tells us that two officials from the contracted anti-doping agency have arrived and are sitting at a nearby table. They are here to conduct an unannounced drug test and have requested that Lucas be available immediately after breakfast.

Team Browne demanded this procedure as one of the terms of agreeing to the fight. Further, it has been stipulated that the testing be conducted by an independent drug-testing organisation, to ensure the integrity of the process. Our team trusts that Lucas is a clean athlete; this testing is about ensuring a level playing field.

The contracted organisation is the Las Vegas–based Voluntary Anti-Doping Association (VADA). The two officials who will conduct the test work directly for the Danish anti-doping service provider Clearidium, which has been contracted by VADA for the sample collection process. The samples will be sent for analysis to the Olympic Testing Laboratory at the University of California in Los Angeles.

The officials now approach our table and inform Lucas that his testing will occur as soon as he is done eating. They take seats at an adjacent table and patiently wait for us to conclude. The notion that these tests are randomly timed is comforting for an athlete and his team who believe that their man is principled and clean. But still, it is a formality to get out of the way so routine can again rule.

Matt and I accompany Lucas up to his room with the two officials, one a woman, the other a man. The first ten minutes or so are spent with the officials laying out their equipment and materials and outlining the details of the testing to Lucas. All along, I am moving about the room taking photos from different angles until the male agent tires of it and instructs me sharply that there are to be no further photos. I manage a few more while Matt stands beside Lucas.

The woman adopts the lead role, the man hovering in the background observing, then accompanying Lucas into the toilet when he provides the urine sample. The process is very clear, the woman quite specific in her instructions.

Lucas sits at the small desk while she stands beside him and, through her stilted English, guides him through the process. She lays out two small vials and two peel-off tags, then asks Lucas to read the tags and sign and date them. One will be blood sample A, the other blood sample B. She straps the tourniquet to his left arm and draws the blood into the first vial and places it on the desktop near Lucas. She attaches the second to the syringe and draws sample B. When the procedure is complete, she instructs Lucas to very firmly fasten the lids to each vial and attach each tag. She then places each blood sample into a small case.

The procedure is repeated for the urine test. Vials are laid out, tags read, signed and dated and Lucas goes into the bathroom followed by the male official. He returns with a urine sample, which is divided into the two vials. They are sealed, labelled and put away. The whole procedure has been conducted with a quiet air of professionalism. The woman hands Matt the documentation for the testing and their own certificates of identity. We note that the man is a Russian national.

Routine is important at this point. It is now Ruslan Chagaev's turn to be tested. He has arrived at the hotel flanked by guards toting automatic weapons and is now waiting down in the foyer. Matt takes the opportunity to slip away, taking a boxing glove down to him. When Matt returns, he is holding a glove bearing the signature of the reigning WBA heavyweight champion and, with the contender's signature on it as well, he believes he has a handy piece of boxing memorabilia. So, unlike the rest of Team 'Big Daddy', Matt has met Chagaev, encountering a quietly spoken and accommodating man.

Back in Australia, the National Rugby League season opens this Thursday evening Australian time with the Parramatta Eels hosting 2015's beaten grand finalists, the Brisbane Broncos. With Lucas being a former Eels player in the age divisions, we are aware that Parramatta plans to promote Lucas's title fight during the game. So Matt takes some photos of Lucas in his Parramatta jersey, his huge arms encircling my neck in a headlock, my face turning as maroon as my Broncos shirt. We'll see who the winner is on Thursday when we hope to listen in to the game online.

Now the Australian press is on Matt's phone, which is encouraging. It is reassuring to consider that some of the sporting press back home have their minds on Lucas and his historic attempt to secure boxing fame. It seems that Brisbane's Alex Leapai received much more coverage than

Lucas when he attempted to lift Wladimir Klitschko's undisputed heavyweight crown in April 2014. Coincidentally, that was taking place at the very same time that Lucas was taking the Commonwealth title in Sheffield.

Alex was taking on the world's very best, a hulking giant of the sport in more ways than the obvious, and he deserved all the publicity he received. Yet it seems some Australian media consider Lucas to be a doomed ship, the Titanic or the Mary Celeste, even before embarking into stormy seas. Matt's phone has been busy; some reporters have been reaching out to the fighter, bunkered down deep here in Grozny. Their efforts are rewarded: Lucas is as natural a talker as he is a fighter. At 11 am Rodney lays out a rope ladder on the carpeted floor of the hallway outside Lucas's room. Further down the hall he places seven or eight plastic cups, upside down in a roughly circular formation. Lucas's agility drills commence for the day, lightly tiptoeing and stepping through the rungs of the floor ladder, forwards, backwards, sideways, over and over again. Then to the cups, with Lucas shadow-boxing, his footwork precise and nimble, seldom upsetting a cup. The session lasts an hour and tests an athlete's aerobic and agility skills.

We sit in the hallway, Lucas, Rodney and I. Rodney regards Lucas as one of the most marketable sportsmen in Australia. His ability, sharp mind and charisma make for a powerful cocktail. A victory in the flaming cauldron of Grozny would add unparalleled achievement to that mix. Lucas is something of a paradox. Complexity, confronting honesty, a need for privacy and a willingness to self-analyse all coexist in him, all at the same time. It is impossible not to listen when this charismatic boxer, four days out from the fight of his life, is willing to talk about himself, and not just about the banal and trite, but things more profound and fundamental. 'Authenticity' is a word that keeps cropping up.

Yet you sense that there is much going on below the surface with this man; you can't help but think that to get to know him he would first have to trust you implicitly. Until then you are reminded of a becalmed ocean surface, giving no hint to the treasures and shipwrecks in its darkened depths.

Within the ring he doesn't trash-talk or aggressively eye-ball opponents; he's too smart to try to fool himself. He goes into the ring believing he has more than enough to get the job done, so there is nothing to be gained by trying to be somebody he is not.

He cannot talk for long about himself or his feelings without his conversation drifting to his family. The highlights of his life are the births of his three children, Angelica, Isaac and Billy. He is well aware another highlight is looming this Saturday night. You sense that he is ready.

Again our conversation returns to the opportunity that lies before Lucas. I suggest that Rodney's name will one day be the answer to a Trivial Pursuit question: 'Who was the trainer of Australia's first ever world heavyweight boxing champion, Lucas Browne?'

We discuss the significance of this fight, not just for Lucas, but also in the context of Australian boxing history. We throw up some watershed moments, fights that seemed to not only excite true boxing fans, but also had social or cultural meaning, capturing the imagination of a nation.

I immediately suggest Lionel Rose's stunning victory over Fighting Harada, a contest that inspired me as a teenager. Here was a nineteen-year-old Indigenous boxer, blessed with raw natural talent, but charmingly naive in the ways of the world, travelling to Tokyo to take on their legend, the mighty Fighting Harada, for the bantamweight championship of the world. All this in 1968, just a year after the Australian national parliament amended its constitution so that Aboriginal people would be included in the census. In winning on foreign soil, Lionel Rose wrote an incomparable page in the history of Australian boxing and returned to Melbourne to find a tumultuous welcome akin to the famed reception given to the Beatles.

We mention Jimmy Carruthers versus Vic Toweel, Jeff Fenech's wars with Azumah Nelson and any of Kostya Tszyu's fights. Matt has now joined us and he draws our attention to the champions of long ago, the Tommy Burns versus Jack Johnson battle in Sydney in 1908. Though neither was Australian, the fight had enormous social and racial ramifications.

Great fights capture the mood of the times in which they happen. They seem iconic in their context, dividing or uniting a nation's people. They can be brutally savage in their execution or artistically and aesthetically pleasing in their strategy, but either way great fights earn their place in history, never to be forgotten. We ponder. Will young men and women one day be talking about the classic Browne–Chagaev fight, the night the Australian became the champ? None of us mentions the possibility of defeat. We believe he will win. We will see.

Abubakar sits alone outside my room, vigilantly scanning the hallway, pistol by his side. The guards have their own room on our twenty-fourth floor and I presume that Shamil and Aslan are there. So I take the opportunity for a photo of one of our Chechen guards with his gun, and try to convey my request to him with hand motions, charades-like. But Abubakar, the mildest-mannered bodyguard you are ever likely to meet, misunderstands me, and now, instead of a camera in my hand, I hold a fully loaded Glock. So this is how you disarm a Chechen bodyguard. You ask him for a picture. Perhaps I was wrong in my judgement of their professionalism, but I think not. I'm sure he could still dismantle me if he so desired, even with me holding the loaded weapon. This is just another contradiction between the omnipresent threat of violence and genuine friendliness and hospitality, Chechen style. So what to do with this loaded gun, but keep my finger away from the trigger and call out excitedly to everyone else. I pose as a cold-blooded hit man, but not very well apparently, as the response on social media is not at all complimentary of my technique. Lucas, on the other hand, goes for the shirt-off pose. He looks the part.

We lunch in the restaurant on the thirty-second floor where the blazing blue sky and warming sun make Moscow seem a distant memory. Our translator, Ibby, is scanning the news on his phone and tells us that Leonardo DiCaprio has won Best Actor at the Academy Awards. I ask him what was awarded best picture and he deliberates, while either he or his phone app interprets from Chechen to English. Finally he informs me that In the Centre of the Light *has won and I am left mystified. I haven't heard of that movie. Perhaps something was lost in translation, as later we learn that Spotlight won the award.*

Lucas spends the afternoon relaxing, while Rodney, Matt and I walk to the beautiful Akhmad Kadyrov Mosque nearby, which can hold 10,000 worshippers at a time, then down through the shopping precinct to the backstreets where swarms of moneychangers flock upon us, walking ATMs. They chatter and surge towards us, but never harass or annoy. Once we have chosen one dealer to negotiate with, the others just look on good naturedly; 7550 Russian roubles for our US$100.

We walk the backstreets of Grozny, down through the laneways and alleyways to the fringes of the market precinct. Lucas and Rodney had taken the same path days ago, Lucas mixing easily with the locals, winning their affection. They ventured deep into the market, which travel websites warn against. The markets are still a couple of hundred metres away when Rodney and Matt enter a shop and, while I wait on the footpath, I notice a man loitering nearby, accompanied by a teenage boy. We move on down the street and they follow some ten metres behind. We pause and they pause. We move on and they move on. The hairs on the back of my neck start to stand up. Suddenly there is a flash of someone quickly approaching from behind and I swivel in time to see the boy brush past me at a sprint across the street to be lost in the crowd. We all turn to look at the man who has been with him, but he can just be seen secreting himself away behind a set of stairs leading into a nearby shop. We retreat back the way we came, not knowing what we had just seen. Most probably we had misinterpreted a father recognising Rodney as Lucas's trainer and sending his son for family to come and join them. Who knows, but retreating seems the prudent option.

We are back at our hotel and Lucas is rested and refreshed. A routine is being established; breakfast at 9 am, agility drills in the hallway outside his room at 11 am, lunch at 2 pm, dinner at 7 pm and a workout in the ring at 9 pm. The ring is in the gym of the Akhmat Fight Club, the production line of Chechen boxing. It is located in a high-security compound, forty minutes' drive from the centre of Grozny.

Our driver, Ruslan, takes the four of us and Ibby in the van, following the car containing our armed security guards. The character of each of our bodyguards is starting to show through, their stern and formal appearance giving way to smiles and fumbling attempts to communicate. We ask which of them is the leader, the best killer, and Abubakar and Aslan immediately point to Shamil, the smallest of them. It is no real surprise; he has that air of being in control. So to us Australians, Shamil is now 'Boss Man', a label he seems to wear with pride.

Our convoy takes us along a highway, past heavily armed military and police, sometimes swarming in groups in the centre of the road, stopping and searching cars, sometimes just a single figure standing randomly in the roadside dark.

The gym is a part of a high-security compound just off the highway, removed from urban lighting or housing. We turn right off the road down a bitumen laneway until we come to the first security gate. Two armed guards permit our entry to this no-man's-land. Two huge statues of ferocious lions pose ominously by the gates. Again we are granted entry, this time to the inner sanctum. The heart of this complex is one of President Kadyrov's palaces, *which explains the level of security. As we wind our way up to the gym we pass a large caged area in which stands a brooding dog, threatening in the murky darkness. Through the tree line we can see other cages, which reportedly have contained wild animals, the big cats, in the president's personal zoo.*

As we enter the foyer of the gym we take off our shoes and walk in our socks on the matted surface. Some other boxers are present but they are doing floor drills or bag work; Lucas has the ring to himself. His workout is impressive, building in intensity as it continues. Moving, bobbing and on his toes, he flicks out his stinging jabs, he rips in with his heavy right-hand artillery, thundering into Rod's pads, sometimes knocking him off balance. His display makes my confidence grow. Rodney varies the work, sometimes using a shortened pool noodle that he waves back and forth, making Lucas bob and weave to avoid being hit. He holds a hit bag to his chest, enticing big uppercuts and rips from Lucas. Lucas is filmed during the whole session, the cameraman swooping like a shark when Lucas slumps to a squat with a jarring pain in that thumb knuckle. We hold our breath, but it's just a stinger and he's back into it.

To complete the day, we learn that Kostya Tszyu will be at the fight, a guest of President Kadyrov. A four-time world champion, he was born in Russia and now lives in Moscow, but for twenty years from 1992 he lived in Australia – surely the Aussie in his spirit still breathes. Perhaps there will be one Russian-accented voice screaming 'C'mon Lucas!' come Saturday night.

As we travel the now quiet highway back into Grozny, we skirt around a large roundabout that controls the flow of traffic into and out of an adjacent shopping centre. On the island that the road circles is a gigantic globe of the Earth, four or five storeys tall. The globe is structurally and aesthetically impressive, but in geographical accuracy it is found wanting. As we drive past, Lucas and Rodney point out that there are two countries of New Zealand shown, two North Islands and two South Islands, depicted side by side. As we drive, I think about the events that I find myself a part of. As long as I can remember, my answer to the parlour-game question of 'what sporting event would you most like to go to?' has always been a world heavyweight title fight. And here I am. I consider my journey here – and the road that Lucas has travelled to arrive here. Questions arise: has the world heavyweight belt always been an alluring goal for him? He wasn't always Lucas 'Big Daddy' Browne. Now there's a question: is there a difference between the boxer 'Big Daddy' and the man Lucas Browne?

II. A Force of Nature

It was Saturday night, 31 July 2010, and, at least for the moment when he stepped into a ring – or even a cage for mixed martial arts events – Lucas Browne had become 'Big Daddy'. The name did its own advertising: 'Come and watch me and be entertained,' it said.

There is something untamed and primeval about this man when he steps into the ring. Outside it, he is contained and in control, coherent and affable, discerning and astute, a man of the times. But born in a different time, in a different place, who can guess what Lucas Browne may have been? Perhaps the answer is hinted at in one of the tattoos decorating his torso: 'I was born to do this'. Browne himself has no doubt: 'No matter where I was in time, I was born to be a combative person, whether a gladiator or a Viking. I was born to do this, to be a warrior.'

Within the ring stands a warrior; outside the ring is an urbane man, but one with an inner part of him slumbering and dormant, that dark, viscous pool of violence, undisturbed and still. There is no switch that he consciously flicks as he takes to the battle to unleash the ferocity within. Lucas Browne and 'Big Daddy' automatically become one identity when they have to be.

Neither Lucas Browne nor 'Big Daddy' is fazed by physical challenge. The ring is a dangerous place – boxers die – but Lucas Browne has seen more danger outside it.

'I've had guns, knives, bottles and chairs thrown at me. I've had three or four blokes on me at the same time,' he explains, referring to his previous life as a bouncer around Sydney. 'To go from all that to a controlled environment, why would I worry? And there's a referee in there if anything did go wrong. It's quite calming for me.'

On that winter evening in 2010, Lucas 'Big Daddy' Browne stood in the cage for his Xtreme mixed martial arts (MMA) fight and looked across at his opponent, the American Daniel Cormier. A champion freestyle wrestler, an Athens Olympian, the 2008 US wrestling team captain at the Beijing Games until ill health denied him living out that honour – Browne had never fought anyone quite like him.

In fact, he had trained for two months to face another fighter from Cormier's stable, Mike Kyle. Kyle was a fighter more inclined to stand up and trade it with his opponent, a style Browne was prepared for. When Kyle withdrew two days out and was replaced by Cormier, Browne faced a totally different challenge, one that turned out to be life-changing.

In the audience that evening were around 150 of his friends, there to support him as he faced his biggest challenge thus far. As was usually the case, his brothers, Danny and Patrick, were among them. But tonight, for the first and only time in his entire fighting career, their father, Graeme, sat with them. The bell sounded.

The two fighters came together and it was on. Browne threw a long left jab that his opponent didn't even seem to see coming. It smacked Cormier right in the mouth, snapping his head back with the heavy impact. The American reacted instinctively by grabbing Browne's leg, levering it and bringing him straight down to the canvas. Suddenly, all advantage was with the American. He had 'Big Daddy' on the canvas where his skills were maximised and Browne's were non-existent. And Browne knew it.

'When it comes to stand-up fighting, I'm very, very good. When it comes to wrestling, I'm rubbish. On my back in a fight, I'm like a turtle.'

Browne would not see the five minutes of that first round out before the referee stepped in. He struggled up from the canvas twice only for the former Olympic wrestler to bring him back down again, hanging on with the relentless death grip of a voracious crocodile. Browne was still throwing punches, still in the fight, but his opponent was dominating the tone of the battle completely through his wrestle.

With about a minute to go in the round, Cormier struck the decisive blow. He came down with a wicked elbow right on the big Australian's left eye, opening the eyebrow up so that it almost flopped down over his line of vision. Blood gushed out of the gaping wound, further hampering Browne's sight. Now he was easy prey, unable to see or evade most of the blows coming his way and, at 4:35 in the round, the referee handed a TKO victory to Cormier.

Browne finished the fight looking pretty busted up. His left ear was purple, his face was swollen, his left eye puffed and split. The eye required thirteen stitches and closed up completely. Not only did he appear well beaten up, he knew he had been.

When he lost to Cormier he had already fought only twice in a professional boxing ring, while this was his sixth time in the cage, with two more fights to come. But the defeat at the hands of this future UFC light heavyweight world champion cemented his realisation that Lucas 'Big Daddy' Browne was a far more lethal fighter standing on his feet than lying on his back.

He dealt with that loss much the same way he dealt with his wins: 'That's done, what's next?' When Lucas 'Big Daddy' Browne is in that ring or cage, that particular fight means everything to him, but once it's done, he moves on to his next target. The defeat made him compare the skills needed in mixed martial arts to the skills he possessed:

I don't want to do anything by halves. If I'm good at this part of something, but not good at that part, it's not good enough for me. I want to do things to the fullest of my capacity.

He wasn't to know it then of course, but that attitude would, less than six years later, take him to faraway Grozny for a tilt at a world heavyweight boxing belt. However, long before the notion of 'Big Daddy' ever occurred to Lucas Browne, sporting success had come to him as a matter of course.

III. Down at Duck Creek

Danny, Lucas and Patrick Browne grew up in a boys' paradise, a neighbourhood full of similar-aged boys, all congregating around the fields, trees and waters nearby. For boys growing up in Granville in Sydney's western corridor in the 1980s, Brussels Street held a particular attraction. It was bordered at one end by a sprawling expanse of parkland, botanical gardens and sports fields. With the sullen waters of Duck Creek meandering through Horlyck Reserve, it was a haven for young boys seeking adventure. Down at Duck Creek, they rode bikes, built skateboard ramps, climbed trees, swung from flying foxes and played bull rush. And across the far side of the languid waterway, they played sport.

They would set out from their rendered fibro house, which was as modest and unpretentious as most in the neighbourhood. What set it apart from the rest were its immaculate lawn, lush gardens and impeccable appearance. Graeme Browne was a house-proud man, someone who enjoyed the company of his family and close friends, but shied away from crowds; he was happiest watching his sons play sport, gardening or up the backyard tending to his pigeons that he loved to race. It was his mum, Leonie, that a young Lucas Browne saw running the daily business of the family home:

> Dad was at everything I did, always very supportive
> in that way. But it was Mum who ran the house.
> If I wanted to go somewhere, or needed help with
> something, or wanted money, I went to Mum.

At ten or eleven years of age Browne was already bigger than most of his peers, not heavier or more thick-set, but certainly taller. And he was to discover that the coordinated sports skills that came so naturally to him had not been gifted to everyone. Whatever sport he turned to, he excelled in: baseball, football, rugby league, basketball and athletics. As a junior soccer player, more than once he received the ball from the kick-off and just belted it from where he stood at the halfway line and scored, the impact of the ball knocking the portable goals over. Once he scored eighteen of the twenty-one goals his team scored in a thrashing of their opponents. On a league field, he scored an astonishing fifty-seven points in one game.

Still, the young boy didn't have an ego to match his ability. His mother, Leonie, recalls a son who enjoyed the game, oblivious to the result: 'As a younger boy, he wasn't competitive at all. His team would win 15-nil and Lucas would come off the field at the end of the game and ask who won.'

Athletics took him to the schoolboy state championships in high jump and he gained rep honours as well in baseball, arguably the most influential of all the sports he played, as far as his future skills in boxing were concerned.

The developing baseballer was predominately a pitcher, and not one with a lot of subtlety to his bag of tricks. Browne remembers it this way: 'I didn't have much of a repertoire in regard to my pitching. I didn't throw any curve balls or anything else, just straight, really fast ones.' That description applied to his early days as a boxer.

Browne believes that the skills he learned pitching a baseball set up the success of his fighting career. The technique of coordinating your feet, body, arms and wrist in one fluent motion for maximum effect with a baseball are directly transferable to landing a power punch in the boxing ring. Browne is of the opinion that the baseball mound is where his right arm power was nurtured: 'It's the action of getting the power from your feet to your hips and your arm following through, following the line of the ball.'

All of Lucas Browne's schooling was through the Catholic system, from Holy Family in Granville as a primary boy to Trinity College at Auburn as a Year 12 student. Always bright and articulate, he had the intelligence and ability to achieve well at school, but as he grew older, an attitude that challenged authority hindered his success:

> I was good at school, but I have always, no matter what, had a problem with authority. I had my own thoughts on everything and thought that my way should be the way it is.

The teenager that he had now become pushed boundaries just because they were there. Where the smoother path would demand respectful observation of rules and self-discipline, he was choosing the rocky track of noncompliance, indifferent to consequences.

And he started to find himself in too many fights in the schoolyard. Even as a young teenager, Browne was never one to back off from anyone, but, equally, he wasn't someone who went looking for a fight:

> I never bullied anyone, but I never got bullied by anyone. I've always hated bullies and if any of my mates got pushed around, I'd stick up for them. I did have a bit of a mouth on me though with the older boys and, when I was in Year 7, I'd end up fighting my brothers' Year 12 mates. I wouldn't be landing any punches, but I'd be kicking their shins and whatever I could. I didn't back down from anyone.

By the time he was fifteen, Lucas Browne was a tall, lanky teenager, wiry and tough. Rugby league was now his sport of choice, playing front row in Parramatta's Harold Matthews under-15 side. But it was the following year in the club's S. G. Ball under-17s when he really hit his straps. Now a big, fast winger, Browne found the try line in most of his games, playing in a team that featured future Parramatta greats Nathan Hindmarsh and Jason Cayless. His potential gained him selection in the club's under-18 side, but Browne didn't play, his league career over, his working life about to begin.

IV. Getting the Job Done

A streak of independence and hot-headedness had Browne leaving the family home just before he was due to complete his schooling and, when he found himself living with friends, it was now time to stand on his own two feet. Browne describes himself as this Jekyll and Hyde character. While he didn't do his HSC exams, he did complete a retail course, topping his form. The other student in the class came second. But, at this stage of his life, he was made for a successful retail career.

This tall, sharp-witted, eloquent young man, not yet tattooed as he is now, found he could engage a customer and sell anything to anyone. He was employed at the menswear store Tony Barlow at Macquarie Shopping Centre, and was soon assistant manager:

> A potential customer walked into the store and told me that he never wore long trousers in his life, but he had to go to a funeral. He walked out again after I sold him a twin trousered suit.

A heavyweight boxer with a background in menswear? Hardly likely, but life has its way of unfolding its own sequence of events, which, when read from the vantage point of hindsight, appears to be an almost predestined way forward. For Browne, the way forward was to leave retail and carve out a career in security.

Now, Browne's alert, astute nature needed to be complemented by physical prowess if he was to be successful in what he did, and he certainly wasn't lacking in that area. Working the clubs and bars from Sydney's Kings Cross out to Parramatta's RSL, he quickly gained a reputation for his competency, coolness under pressure and his ability to get the job done.

He rapidly rose to management level, directing and leading the security teams. Browne always possessed an intuitive ability to read people and situations, an almost sixth sense for when trouble was brewing. And when it did, he was usually the first in, doing whatever had to be done to deal with the situation. He found himself in many, many fights, and most troublemakers found themselves a lot worse off for the experience. It may be a little consolation for their egos if they knew that their dental bills were courtesy of a future heavyweight boxer. But one night, at the Revesby Workers Club, maybe for the first and only time in his life, standing his ground was not an option for Lucas Browne.

The club, out in the Bankstown area of Sydney, had a large patronage and Browne led a security team of up to thirty guards over a weekend. He had taken up a position on an upper floor, from which he had a clear field of vision of most of what was going on below. He trusted his instincts and his ability. 'I'm in my absolute element when I am in charge and in control. I'm extremely good at what I do, a very good observer of people.' What he observed that night was a scuffle brewing. Through his clipped-on microphone Browne directed members of his team to move in closer to the scene and contain the situation. This they did, focusing on the two main combatants, grabbing both and walking them out through the front doors to the footpath. It was clear to Browne that the smallest spark could reignite this fire:

They were trash-talking each other the entire time. We got them out the front of the club and all the boys with them also came out. And just like that, a big punch-up

started, a real free-for-all. We were just starting to get
on top of them when bang, a shot rang out.

When he watched the footage on CCTV later, he would
see the gun tumble to the footpath during the all-in, but at
the time he was too busy mixing it to notice. He would see
one of the gang reach down among the brawl and pick up the
pistol, then fire it into the awning above their heads. He would
also see the gunman lower and twist the weapon sideways,
American mobster style, and let loose four or five shots.

At the time he saw very little at all for, instinctively, he
turned and ran towards the other side of the road as soon as
the shooting started. As he ran with other security guards and
some of the fighters, the pistol coughed repeatedly and bullets
fizzed past. The young man running beside Browne suddenly
stumbled and fell, a round smacking into his leg. Now
writhing on the ground in pain from the gunshot wound, he
had been involved in the original scuffle. The gunman, still
with the weapon in hand, and some of his associates jumped
into a nearby cab and got out of there. As they did so, Browne
had a chaotic situation to secure before the police arrived to
take control of the crime scene. He had a fellow staff member
injured in the brawl, up to thirty other security staff and
upwards of 600 patrons whose safety needed to be ensured,
not to mention a gunshot victim on the street nearby. It made
for a long, stressful night. The shooter and his friends weren't
finished for the night either. They bashed the cab driver and
stole his taxi.

Later Browne would recall noticing something stunning
in those split seconds when bullets were flying and his life

was at risk. As he and just about everyone else ran as fast as they could away from the gunfire, he caught a glimpse of two soldiers who happened to be at the club calmly walking towards the source of the shots. Instinct tells you to flee danger; training tells you to deal with it.

Life was full-on for Browne by now. He was married, with children, and worked long hours in some stressful situations. He arrived home at three or four in the morning and would grab a couple of hours' sleep before helping get his kids to school. He would then catch a bit more sleep before the afternoon routine of collecting the kids, sports training, helping with homework – all the tasks that every parent deals with. And then it was off to security work again. In his late twenties, his marriage failed and his family left Sydney for Perth.

Browne had reached a low point, his life turned upside down, suddenly alone, separated from the people who gave him meaning. His children were, and still are, the centre of his life, the reason he strives to be the best man he can be:

> Once I had children I became a lot wiser about who I
> am. There's a saying about being the person that you
> needed to have in your life when you were younger.
> That's what I've wanted to be for my children, a
> complete and utter role model.

But now, a door had slammed shut in his life. In his loneliness and relative idleness, another door opened. He would enter a mixed martial arts cage and, soon, the persona 'Big Daddy' would be born.

V. Walk the Earth Fearing No Man

'I thought mixed martial arts would be my thing, with my mentality coming from the street in security. I was devastating and very quick because I knew I had to be.'

In many ways cage fighting felt like a natural progression from what Browne was doing five or six nights a week, except now there would be a referee to control the situation. Suddenly with time on his hands, he found himself in a gym, admittedly for only a couple of hours a week. He began working out with a friend who promoted cage-fighting events in Sydney and somehow convinced the friend to put him on his next card.

His eyes weren't fixed on some far-off goal, a reward at the end of a distant journey. On the contrary, Browne just wanted to prove himself in a cage and win a belt, any belt. So not long before his thirtieth birthday, he found himself matched up against Jeff King at Sydney's Luna Park, in February 2009. First-time nerves didn't even come into it. 'I literally fell asleep on the lounge in the change room. They had to wake me up for the fight.'

King managed to wake Browne up once the fight started. He smacked him with a heavy right hand and Browne thought to himself 'good, let's get started'.

He let his instincts take over and responded with a few telling elbows and solid hooks and rips. In the second round, Browne got on top of King and let loose with a flurry of blows. The referee stepped in. He had a win to his name. His fight career had started.

King had come from the stable of Tama Te Huna, who immediately signed up Browne and became his first boxing trainer. Two weeks later Browne found himself in a kickboxing fight with absolutely no idea what to do except punch. This he did, winning in the fourth round.

It was around this time that the idea of 'Big Daddy' was conceived. Like a product being sold in the marketplace, a fighter needs a label, a brand name that not only brings recognition, but also captures his essence. Being the father of three children and with his size, 'Big Daddy' fit like a glove. So for his very first venture into a boxing ring, in March 2009, he fought as Lucas 'Big Daddy' Browne.

But before his boxing career really got into full swing, he was to have a total of eight MMA fights for six wins and two losses. Less than a month after the defeat to the future UFC world champion Daniel Cormier, Browne fought a kickboxer from New Zealand, Sam Brown, and knocked him out in the second round. Once again he found himself thinking he could give cage fighting a red-hot go.

But then he fought the tough New Zealander Jim York. Browne is a strong man, but in York he had met his match:

> He was without doubt the strongest person I have ever
> dealt with in my life. I cracked him one and wobbled him.
> So he grabbed me and I just thought 'wow'. He hit me
> with a left hook and pulled me to the ground. He wasn't a
> wrestler, but, with his strength, he was good at wrestling.

After the York loss, Browne knew boxing better suited his skill set. In all his cage fights he had launched a total of two kicks and won all six victories by power punches. But mixed martial arts had given him a new focus in life. It was after his very first cage fight that people had started asking questions about the big man, wanting to know more about this power puncher. That's when the idea of 'Big Daddy' started to be hatched. It was also when one of his quintessential tattoos was added to his body.

Browne has always liked tattoos, getting the first at seventeen. Many of the tribal symbols that decorate his chest, back and arms are just that, patterns and body art that appeal to him. But running down his spine is the prophetic 'walk the earth fearing no man'. If ever a motto captured the spirit of a warrior, it is this. In its brevity it says all that needs to be said about Lucas 'Big Daddy' Browne and his journey in life.

Of more personal significance are three tattoos, one on his right fist, one on his neck and one over his heart. These are for his three children. And a tattooed tear under his right eye for his father. Uncharacteristically, these tattoos put a very private part of Browne's personal life on public display.

Not many people get to really know Lucas Browne. At times he can be disarmingly honest and polite, while at others he is confronting and profane. On the one hand he is an extremely engaging and affable individual, commanding attention in any room in which he stands, not only by his physique and stature, but more so through his powerful personality. And on the other, he is deeply private, shutting people out at times, dealing with the chaos and darkness that life sometimes sweeps upon us, standing alone on his own two feet. 'There are two different sides to me,' he explains:

It's almost this Lucas Browne and 'Big Daddy' thing.
It's what people expect, this warm, articulate, humble

man and he exists. It's who I am. But away from the crowds and the cameras I can just be Lucas Browne the man, and sometimes, it's not the best. It is who I am.

Browne can be so self-aware and introspective that it can almost work against him in terms of the way he judges himself: 'I can go off on random tangents and devastate my world in ten minutes and come back to where I started and think everything is fine.'

Browne talks about a well of anger that lies deep within him, a reserve that can feed the fighter inside the ring. But if it seeps to the surface in his private life, it can overshadow him and emotionally hurt those who love him. At this deepest level, he is someone who needs other people:

I still have fears, still have self-doubts, still have some issues, I still need to be loved, to have affection; I need a woman in my life, who can see the good in me, almost like reassurance.

Lucas 'Big Daddy' Browne is impossible to ignore, whether you are a boxing fan or not. He defies stereotyping: just when you feel you have captured the essence of his personality, your notions can suddenly seem grossly inadequate or inaccurate. He is the fierce combatant whose physicality is matched by his intellect.

In media interviews or in conversation generally, there are no hackneyed sportsman's cliches; rather, sincere, self-admonishing appraisals expressed in fluent, insightful language. There's an old saying in boxing: you don't really know your true self until you step inside a ring. It's the loneliest sport. Apart from the referee, just you and your opponent stand in that ring and all you really have to draw upon is your inner strength, the person you are deep within. Many fail that test. Browne has passed it time and time again as he draws upon not only that pool of violence, but also his profound identification as a warrior. And like any true warrior, it is in the challenge, and the defeat of his adversary, that he finds fulfilment.

I like watching my opponent's eyes as he starts the fight full of hope and anger. Then I get so much satisfaction watching those same eyes turn to fear as his will slowly fades and he accepts the inevitable. That is when I am at my best, my happiest, when I'm most content and am my true self. It is when the fire in my soul comes out my eyes and fixes on my opponent as I beat his will to the ground.

Confronting, raw, brutal, without doubt: but, equally, honest, lucid and uncompromising.

So from those early days in Brussels Street, from the times pitching a baseball in school days, from selling suits, from the street fights and gunshots of security work, from marriage and the joy of fatherhood and the misery of separation, from the split eyes, bruises and victories and losses of cage fighting, Lucas 'Big Daddy' Browne emerged. Now the boxing world was sitting up and taking notice.

CHAPTER FOUR

A Chechen Story

I. Grozny Chronicle – Tuesday, 1 March 2016

The routine continues with breakfast in the dining room on the third floor. Again, we sit together at the small table, sharing casual conversation and checking social media. At a nearby table sit our shadows, our three bodyguards, breakfasting and appearing as casual as anyone else. Further away sit three other members of Lucas's extended team. There is Philippe, the high-level operator, the man who promises to be a vital cog in the machine come Saturday night when he will attend to any cuts or swellings. For the moment his attention is elsewhere, dealing with the problems and issues that the general public are usually oblivious to and which are best kept from the boxer.

Before breakfast one such drama arises; the details concerning the pay-per-view hook-up to the satellite connection were still unavailable, threatening the coverage of the fight to the wider world. Philippe stews, all the while acting as the conduit between our camp, the promoters and all other vested interests, a task dependent upon his diplomacy and communication skills.

Philippe had a dental practice in Brussels before boxing took over his life. It reminds me of an Irish undertaker I once met in Belfast. He was also a paramedic and played the Irish whistle at wakes. Whatever happened, he couldn't lose – like a dentist who manages boxers.

For now, Philippe sits removed from our Australian team, in the company of his own team, which comprises two others. Sitting opposite him is Dr Georgi Ezekiev, a Bulgarian surgeon whose duty is to attend to any health issues Lucas may encounter now or in the fight. Alongside him is Alexandre Komurian, a French trainer who will provide assistance to the team in any way he can. They sit in quiet conversation while, back at our table, I contentedly sip my flat white, Matt his apple juice, Lucas his green tea and Rodney indulges in his weakness, sweet cakes, as an after-breakfast treat.

At 11 am, with four days to go, Lucas is back on the ladder and cup drills on our twenty-fourth floor. Quiet conversation weaves its way through the session as Lucas, Rod and I sit in the hallway. Lucas is a fighter by trade, but he has just stepped and tiptoed with the agility of a gymnast. A fighter needs to be graceful as well as brutal. Now Lucas speaks to me about his future. When he speaks, you listen.

If he lets you into his world, it's very easy to know and like this man. He doesn't seek great wealth, but, like a man who has known harder times, he wants security. A four-bedroom home, a new car and certainty for his family would be more than enough. We talk about legacy in life, how your values, character and deeds can light the path for those who will follow you, especially your children. What you do in life is important; you are remembered more for who you are, for better or worse.

That's how sportspeople are remembered. I throw in the name of Steve Waugh, the tough, uncompromising Australian Test cricket captain. Without doubt, cricket lovers recall his great centuries and match-winning innings, but what stands out most in retrospect is the character that oozed out of each one. There always seemed a pride, a will and a fighting spirit in that man, a force that wouldn't be denied. Sitting in that hallway, Rodney and I believe Lucas to be that sort of man, about to play a back-against-the-wall innings in a hostile environment. He will triumph because of what he can do and because of who he is. At least I hope so.

I then mention a movie I watched on the plane on the way to Moscow, about the cyclist Lance Armstrong, called The Program. I reflect with Lucas and Rodney on how Armstrong's systematic cheating by the use of performance-enhancing drugs has forever tarnished the man, reduced his legacy to dust. Lucas talks about how he wants to be thought of as an athlete. The label he already proudly wears is that of a 'power puncher', a fighter whose best weapons can knock over any opponent in the world, if he manages to find his target. But he also seeks acknowledgement for being single-minded; a boxer who never took short cuts, one who achieved through focused determination and hard work.

Lucas likes to have people around him and soon family will complete the circle. He learns that his brothers, Danny and Patrick, and friend and sponsor Matt Meyerhoff are on their way to Grozny, from Dubai via Moscow.

With each day, we experience more and more the warmth and good humour of the Chechen people. It's also a place where things out of the ordinary happen. Before Matt and I arrived, Lucas has seen video footage on Boss Man's phone of him firing RPG rounds – that's rocket-propelled grenades, usually rockets tipped with an explosive warhead, used against tanks. Naturally the big man wants a piece of that action. That turns out be a bridge too far, even in Grozny, as Boss Man, looking a little bemused, shakes his head, no. But the idea of firing a weapon has been brewing ever since Lucas saw that footage, and Boss Man and Adam, who has returned for another stint interpreting, have been working behind the scenes trying to make it happen. So, after lunch, the word spreads on the twenty-fourth floor that we are off to an indoor shooting range.

Our driver, Ruslan, opens the sliding door to our van and in get Lucas, Rodney, Matt, me, Philippe, Alexandre, Ibby, Adam and our mandatory three bodyguards. It's no more than a five-minute drive from Grozny City Hotel to the shooting range, which is located in a basement below an arcade of shops. We walk in past a shop window displaying a huge stuffed wolf, forever fixed in its stance, down a winding staircase to the cavernous rooms below.

The unloaded weapons are laid out on a table before us, Glock, Smith & Wesson and a Saiga, together with pistols whose names and origins I have no knowledge of. Lucas chooses a Glock and, donning earmuffs, he is led to a line one-third of the way down the firing range. At the other end stand two rows of heads and torsos and, behind them, the more challenging target, a row of eight smaller heads. The *instructor pushes the clip into the chamber and Lucas has a loaded pistol. He is guided to hold the gun in two hands and take a relaxed, knees-bent stance. I'm beside Lucas taking photos, but the instructor motions for me to move back 5 metres behind the big man. This unexpected workplace health and safety regulation lasts all of thirty seconds as most of our party move forward around Lucas.*

He fires off his first round and the percussion is enormous, even through our muffs, and the recoil of the weapon has his hands hurtling upwards. The shot misses the target. Lucas learns quickly and adjusts for the gun's kick – and target after target falls. Like most elite sportspeople, his skills are transferable to other disciplines. He proves to be a fine shot.

Soon everyone has an opportunity to showcase their skills, but Philippe proves to be the marksman of the group, being the experienced hunter that he is. Matt selects his weapon of choice, a Saiga, a Russian-produced semi-automatic assault rifle. As Matt fires off single rounds in quick succession, targets drop and dispensed shells shower me in my photographer's position nearby. I fire off two rounds and manage to hit the back wall.

I think to myself that this firing range has been a great idea. It wasn't all about proving skills and chest-thumping, though there was some of that. Importantly, it seems to have relaxed a little bit of pressure. Some laughter at this point can only be a good thing. And somehow along the way, our Chechen guards have joined in the laughter, become part of all that is happening. Rodney is teaching them swear words and Aussie slang, Boss Man is 'threatening' to shoot Lucas if he has to and where there was once a barrier of formal politeness, there is now good humour, genuine warmth and some Aussie–Chechen shenanigans. The band of Chechen supporters for Lucas 'Big Daddy' Browne is growing.

On the road out to Akhmat gym this evening there is even more military, stopping cars, searching for rebels or militants. Gun-toting uniformed men congregate at traffic lights and intersections, brandishing their weapons, walking in the laneways, waving down vehicles, sometimes ordering drivers out of their cars.

We learn that here in Chechnya it is illegal for a car to have tinted windows, as this obstructs vision into the interior where gunmen or terrorists may be secreted away. Thankfully we are waved through all the checkpoints. I'm not certain whether it is our bodyguards' doing or because the military are expecting us, but, whichever it is, we are grateful not to have our nerves tested further or for Lucas's routine to be disrupted by security issues.

The gym this evening is quieter and more subdued than last night; we have it almost to ourselves. Matt and I stand on the apron as Lucas and Rodney take to the ring, the routine very similar to yesterday. Their workout tonight is not as intense, stopping at times for easy talk and laughter. There is a relaxed rhythm to the session, but they still work out together with the balance and coordination of graceful ballroom dancers. Momentum is building.

Back in my hotel room, I sit at my laptop and record the events of the day. The title fight looms, an approaching train in a darkened night, one you can hear rumbling in the distance, but one you still cannot see. That rumble – it portends destruction for one fighter, deliverance for the other. My thoughts turn to the Chechens who have entered our lives. Adam, our translator, is enigmatic. He is twenty-eight years old. A moment's reflection on the maths and it is clear that so much of his life has been lived amid war and its shadow. Yet here he is, an educated, sophisticated man. I wonder what it must be like to live through war and how you can come out the other end with your dignity and optimism intact. What has life been like for him?

II. A Time of Survival

Sometimes we are no more than leaves blown before a storm, swept up by the howling winds and scattered without design. All semblance of order is shattered by the randomness of awesome, elemental forces. Those who lived through the storm of war that engulfed Chechnya during the 1990s and the early years of this new millennium were prey to such vicissitudes.

This was war at its most brutal and indiscriminate. Chechen civilian casualties were horrendous. Those who survived the twin conflicts with Russia witnessed the worst that humans can do. They also witnessed the complete destruction of their capital city, Grozny. To survive those years and emerge at the other end still nurturing hope and trust, still being capable of tenderness and love, is quite some achievement. This is Adam Saidov's story. This is how he has lived his life since the war.

When it all started, he was just a child, preoccupied with the concerns of childhood. And when it all ended many years later, he had grown to be a man, one who had survived intact.

His home was Duba-Yurt, a village that lies in the highlands, just thirty or so kilometres south of Grozny. It is cradled into the beautiful Argunsky Gorge, protected on two sides by imposing mountains, its verdant fields and pastures rich and fertile. Duba-Yurt itself stretches from these lower-lying regions to the higher grounds of the mountain district, its 1300 homes located in perhaps the most scenic setting in all of the Chechen Republic. The River Argun, churning and gushing as it accelerates through the gorge, completes the idyllic Garden of Eden atmosphere of the village, the place that the six-year-old boy, Adam, called home.

For a young boy growing up, there were fields to explore, trees to climb, a rope suspension bridge to cross and imperial trout to catch in the Argun. Adam would come home after playing with his friends, home to a large house with a kitchen that opened out to a lush garden. There his family grew most of their own fruit and vegetables, with the fertile soil and mild climate of summer ideal for agriculture. With the onset of winter, they preserved fruits and made pickles. Adam was blessed not only by the natural beauty that surrounded him each day but also by the loving family that he shared his life with.

His father was named Nurdin, Arabic for 'light of belief' and thanks to Stalin's genocide he was born into a family in exile, in Kazakhstan in 1956. Adam's mother, Zara, was born in 1965 and, before the Russian assault upon Chechnya, worked at an ice-cream factory. Adam's elder brother, Islam, was born in 1984 and his sister, Iman, in 1986 and together, this Chechen family of five knew love, security and a belief in the future. Adam was the youngest, born in 1988, and, like his peers the world over, perhaps favour and reward came his way a little more readily than for his siblings.

Theirs was not a life of hardship. Their house was big by local standards and, at a time when generally only government officials owned a car, they had a Volga. Nurdin was a businessman and an antiquarian, a passionate student of history with a zeal for the artefacts, manuscripts and other empirical evidence that support it. The Saidov home was a place of learning, where knowledge and enlightenment were highly valued, a place where stories were told and dreams nurtured.

A Chechen tradition is to gather at a family home, all the extended family, brothers, sisters, grandparents, and share a meal and discuss the happenings of the day. The Saidovs were no different. Into Nurdin and Zara's home came Nurdin's three brothers and two sisters and their partners and they all sat around one large table, at the head of which was their father, Adam's grandfather. As is custom, due honour and respect was paid to the eldest man, at the head of the table.

His name was Hamid Saidov. He was a survivor. He was of the Chechen generation rounded up by Stalin for extermination or deportation. Hamid, along with everyone he knew, every living Chechen and neighbouring Ingush that the Soviets could find, was detained and forcibly evicted from his home, his village, his country.

He recalled the panic among his countrymen and -women as they were herded like cattle to the railway yards and loaded into stock carriages, crammed so closely together that there was no place to sit, the wailing of frightened children failing to penetrate the hardened hearts of Soviet guards. Hamid long remembered the voice of one old man who brought calm to that cattle carriage. 'Do not be afraid,' he urged. 'We will not be brought there where Allah is absent.' Their faith would survive and give them strength.

Many perished however. The frigid cold of February was their enemy, its icy fingers slipping easily through the gaps in the boxcars, piercing the hearts of the old, the young and the infirm. When the train finally ground to a halt those that had survived the journey found themselves at a railway siding in Kazakhstan. They had reached their destination, the cold flat plains of central Asia, their place of exile for at least the next thirteen years. Starvation and exposure would claim the lives of many, perhaps up to a half of the total number of Chechens and Ingush, including a number of Hamid's own family.

It would be here, in exile, that Hamid would meet and marry Adam's grandmother and together they would have six children, three born in Kazakhstan, including Nurdin, and three more born in their native land, Chechnya.

Four years after the death of Stalin in 1953, the first of the exiled peoples were permitted to return to their native lands. But it would be another three years again until Hamid Saidov would lead his family back in 1960 to their patrimonial home, Duba-Yurt. He, his family and many of his fellow Chechens had not looked upon their homeland for sixteen long years. His burden of unfathomable hardship was over. He had survived.

Many years later, in 1994, he would sit at the head of that table and share dinner and daily news with his family. He was not to know then that the time of peace was about to be shattered. Russian president Boris Yeltsin would bring the Russian foot down on Chechen moves for independence, and the consequences would be catastrophic.

III. A Time of War

Adam was just six years old when the lanterns started falling from the sky. As they floated to earth on their tiny orange parachutes, they shone brightly, fascinating the children of the village. In the morning they would go around the fields and roads of their town, collecting them from their resting places, some dangling from the tree branches or wires that broke their fall. It wasn't until some of the adults intervened that the children of Duba-Yurt began to understand the real purpose of these lamps from the sky.

'It is a warning from the Russians,' they were advised. 'They drop them from their planes to tell us to leave our homes. It is psychological pressure.'

The children were not quite correct; these objects certainly were not just pretty lamps falling in a night sky. But the adults were not quite right either; these objects were not just psychological weapons. Their purpose was much more sinister. These 'lanterns' were not lamps at all, but bright markers, target-setting beacons that Russian aircraft and machine-gun crews could zero in on. Soon outlying villages like Duba-Yurt would come under Russian assault, but, for now, bombing raids on the village were sporadic; the battle for Grozny raged 30 kilometres away.

The shelling and rocket fire upon the Chechen capital was ferocious. The sounds of the battle reverberated up through the gorge to the village where Adam lived, and the occasional Russian jetfighter brought destruction to their doorstep. Many of the fathers, including Nurdin Saidov, had left Duba-Yurt to take up arms in defence of their homeland. Now the old men, the women and the children sought refuge from the war that was creeping ever closer, in an underground cellar belonging to one of Adam's uncles. With its thick fortified concrete walls, it acted as a bunker, a bomb shelter from the assault that was surely coming.

There, in that cellar, Adam, his family and some other villagers lived for several months. They left their refuge only occasionally in the late afternoon, when there was a lull in the fighting in Grozny. They were not to know that Russian troops had begun their approach into the mountainous regions of the Shalinsky district, targeting townships like Duba-Yurt.

One night, for whatever reason, Adam's family did not return to the cellar. That very night, the Russian military turned its wrath upon Duba-Yurt.

The assault upon the village was brutal and fearsome. A time that Adam still remembers as 'the most terrible night of my life' had begun. As Adam's mother huddled with her three children inside their home, artillery fire and rocket attacks turned the village into an inferno, visiting death and destruction on the town. This former Garden of Eden echoed with the whine of shells and the thud of explosions;

it glowed with white-hot metal splinters arcing through the air; it reeked of burning houses. When the air cleared, whole families lay slaughtered; the little bodies of Adam's childhood friends lay dead and disfigured.

The Saidovs and their house had survived the torrid assault. The plain fact of the obscenity of war lay before them, fusing in the smouldering ruins of their once beautiful town and festering in the now-still bodies of its victims. Nurdin, who was in the village at the time, led his family out of the wreckage of Duba-Yurt and took them to the relative safety of a more isolated refuge, the mountain village of Hacharoy, near the border with Georgia.

There, his family found respite from the war that still raged, a war that he himself still fought. Adam, Islam, Iman and their mother, Zara, lived in the small, cosy home of a generous lady named Yakha. The widow of Nurdin's best friend, she welcomed the asylum seekers with an open heart, providing them with shelter for the next four months until the war with Russia concluded. Adam recalls this time in the majestic mountains around Hacharoy as a time of tranquil beauty, picking wild strawberries, riding a horse; there was no radio, no TV, no electricity, only cows, nature and pure mountain air. And only the occasional zoom of an overhead jet to remind him of war. But by the end of 1996, the skies too fell silent. Grozny had been retaken by Chechen forces and the Russians would soon withdraw.

The family returned home to Duba-Yurt. Their home still stood, just pockmarked by shell fragments. They were greeted by tears from relatives and friends: the Saidovs were believed lost, but here they were, alive. The time of war was over.

IV. A Time of Nightmares

The time following the war held some promise for the Saidov family and for Chechnya generally. Life was readjusting its rhythms to the conditions of peace, though the eruption of bombs and the bark of gunfire was a constant reminder that stability had not returned to their country and lawlessness had cast its menacing shadow over the land.

But the Russian troops had completely disengaged from Chechnya and a formal peace agreement had been signed – even if the question of independence was not settled. Presidential elections were held in 1997 and a new parliament was formed. Green shoots of hope had begun to sprout among the residual rubble of war. For a family like Adam's, there was reason for optimism. In wider Chechnya, however, the rule of law had broken down. The institutions that stabilise society were sagging. Some veterans of the brutal conflict with Russia knew little else now but the power of a gun; warlords and religious zealots were determined to cling to their power.

Chechen society and the independence movement were split. Foreign fighters from neighbouring Arab nations, with their more extreme ideologies and religious beliefs, entered the country. In the Chechnya of the late nineties there was no politician or military leader firmly in charge; leadership and decision-making was fractured. A Russian envoy to Chechnya was kidnapped and killed at Grozny airport, announcements about the phasing in of Islamic religious law were made and apartment blocks were bombed.

People were being killed in Russia too in 1999. Almost 300 people perished when apartment blocks in three cities were bombed in September. When a fifth bomb was found before it detonated, the then prime minister Vladimir Putin ordered the bombing of Chechnya. The second Chechen war had begun. Within days it became apparent the fifth bomb had been planted by Russia's own spies, who claimed it was a training exercise. Many Russians, including MPs, believed Putin was orchestrating war to ensure he was elected president. Too late – the wheels of war could not be stopped.

This time Russia waged total war. The Saidovs once more were drawn into the nightmare of history. Grozny was to be razed. By February of the new millennium the Russians had achieved their goal. They had captured Grozny, a smouldering ruin, a horrific vision of Hades on Earth. Soon enough, Putin's forces turned their attention to outlying regions, villages like Duba-Yurt, where fighters lurked.

Adam's father, Nurdin, did not fight in the second war. In the first conflict he fervently wore the military uniform of his homeland, but this war was different. Religious extremism and factional agendas had taken the place of sound military judgement. If the first war was a war for soldiers and patriots, this war was one for zealots and gang leaders. Nurdin decided to get his family out of Duba-Yurt. He had no choice but to leave them in the village while he travelled to the Russian city of Saratov, almost 1000 kilometres away, to make arrangements for their escape.

At the same time, Zara left her children with her sister while she journeyed to Rostov – 800 kilometres and a world away – to work, earning what she could for the family. It was then that the Russians attacked their village.

Just like in the first war five years before, the people of the village had been witnesses to the cataclysmic attack upon Grozny. The sounds of battle, the roar of jets and the pall of smoke told their own story. But no one expected the barbarism that was to come. Surely a warning for civilians to depart the village would precede any assault. But no such warning came. What did come, however, was a fleet of low-flying MiG-29 jet fighters.

Adam, now twelve years old, was at school that day, just he and one other boy in the classroom with the teacher. He saw the jets long before he heard them. They came in through the Argunsky Gorge, flying so low that they barely cleared the treetops. From the schoolroom window Adam could clearly see the rockets that the first MiG ejected, seemingly directed at his classroom. The explosion was horrendous, missing his classroom, but tearing into the walls, desks, books and bodies of a room nearby. The distinctive screech and gnashing of metal being ripped apart has stayed in Adam's mind from that day. Mixed with the scream of the jet engines as the fighter soared away, the cacophony of destruction drowned out the rest of the world. Adam found himself alive, under a classroom desk, when the initial impact subsided.

His teacher acted on instinct and led Adam and his classmate out of the burning classrooms and onto the street. Here she told them to run home. Before he obeyed, Adam asked her innocently, 'And when do we come back to school again?'

The teacher's face, eyes until then wide with fear and shock, now softened into a smile. 'When the war is over,' she replied.

With the war now raging, Zara Saidov could not return home. The Russian fist had Chechnya by the throat and the movement of civilians was heavily restricted. Similarly Adam's father was trapped in Saratov. So Adam, along with his brother and sister, lived for eight months in his aunt's home. Food was scarce and hardships were endured by all, but family was still family and together they survived. Yet still the bombardment of Duba-Yurt continued.

One night was worse than all the others. Artillery shells rained down upon the village, bringing indiscriminate ruin and death. So many of those shuddering explosions, with their furnace heat and fizzing metal, sounded as if they were just outside their feeble wooden front door. The four of them, Islam, Iman, Adam and their aunt, sought refuge in their bathtub. Cowering together, they held grimly to life and to each other as the shelling continued.

In the bathtub Adam cried. The whine of each incoming shell seemed like a harbinger of doom. Adam prayed to Allah, asking only one thing: to once again see the faces of his parents. But among the carnage and terror, trembling in that bath, with war screaming outside his walls, a great truth visited Adam, a truth that he would never forget: 'Great happiness requires not really very much, only to realise that you still live.'

The next morning Duba-Yurt lay in ruins. Old men and women, their faces blank with shock, aimlessly shifted through the debris where once stood their homes. One woman stood and stared, hands to her face, a cat forlornly clinging to her legs, her couch that once sat guests and family now strewn with dust and splintered timber. The Russians controlled the village, roads in and out were blocked; the Chechens were prisoners in the smoking rubble.

Eventually civilians were permitted to leave the ruin of their town and Adam's aunt, Adam himself, Islam and Iman joined the human stream of displaced Chechen villagers as they sought refuge in the higher regions nearby.

Together they trudged, all in one direction, away from the Russian troops, higher and deeper into the mountainous regions. Many stopped and turned, searching the faces of others intently, hoping to recognise a loved one. Among them were the elderly, carried on stretchers and in wheelchairs hastily constructed from boards and old bicycle wheels.

Adam came across a family of three men, obviously a grandfather, his son and his grandson, the youngest being about sixteen and named Uvays. The grey-haired grandfather was borne on a stretcher by his two descendants. They stopped to talk. Smiling, the father addressed Islam and Adam and told them that the grandfather had tried to persuade them to leave him behind. Then, winking at them in a manner of one who is about to divulge a secret, he turned to the old man and scolded him playfully. 'Here, if you married the neighbour Bayset when we asked you to, then we could have safely entrusted you to her.'

The grandfather snapped back at his son, 'Well, you would now also drag two. Rejoice that you only carry one.'

All around, there was laughter. Amid the misery, a moment of happiness flickered past, like the fleeting shadow of a darting bird. By the evening, when the sun had slipped below the horizon, they arrived at the village of Adam's grandmother.

Her home was a place of refuge for many. She sheltered not only Adam's aunt and her nephews and niece, but many other relatives of her extended family and many strangers, refugees from the far corners of the republic. Sometimes, in times of war, the true heroes reside far from the front lines. Eventually came the joyous day when Adam's mother, Zara, returned and together they resided in his grandmother's house for several months, a short oasis of peace.

One day, word arrived that the Russian troops stationed around Duba-Yurt had granted the villagers passage back to their homes to collect valuables and whatever goods survived that night of chaos. So back they trekked, their hearts filled with trepidation about what they may encounter, their minds haunted by the visions of that terrible night.

They arrived at Duba-Yurt. Soldiers were posted at an entrance point into the village and, after sighting their documentation, waved the Saidovs through. The village was no longer there. In shocked silence, they meandered through the rubble and debris, bricks, timber and metal, strewn and scattered. The shells and rockets had done their job. They ghosted down their now desolate street, not recognising the ruin in front of them as their former home, passing right by it. Turning back, they recognised it. It was destroyed, its memories violated, its meaning vaporised. There was nothing there for them, no family photos, no documents, no property, nothing. They turned away.

In a week's time, a car arrived. The driver had been sent by Adam's father, Nurdin. The driver was there to collect the Saidov family, and he would drive them out through war-torn Chechnya into the deep south of Russia to Saratov, the port city on the Volga. Just a few years before, it was a closed city, the site of a facility manufacturing jet fighters, perhaps the very MiGs that were deployed in the bombings of Duba-Yurt. But for now, it was the city of refuge sought out by Nurdin Saidov for his family. He had purchased a house for them and the car that had delivered them from the conflict. The large Germanic population of the Volga River port provided a community in a Russian city, most accepting of a fleeing Chechen family.

It would not be until April 2009 that Russia would declare its offensive against Chechen rebels over. Before then, many more Russian soldiers and Chechen civilians would perish. In 2002, Chechen rebels would seize a Moscow theatre and hold over 800 people hostage, more than 120 of them dying in the Russian operation to free them. In May 2004, the Russian-backed Chechen president, the former chief mufti of the district of Ichkeria, Akhmad Kadyrov, would be assassinated in a bomb blast in Grozny. Three years later, his son Ramzan Kadyrov would be installed as president by Vladimir Putin.

But for now, in Saratov, the war was far distant. For Adam and his family, a time of nightmares had passed. In years to come, Adam and President Kadyrov would be drawn by fate to the same boxing ring in Grozny.

V. A Time of Dreams

It was just after seven o'clock in the evening of 5 March 2016 and Adam sat in the back of a limousine as it drifted quietly, and as unobtrusively as a stretch limo can, through the city centre streets of Grozny. Dressed smartly in a tailored grey suit, white shirt and black tie, he looked every bit the urbane, sophisticated young man that he had grown to be. Sitting directly to his right was Lucas Browne, the contender on his way to the fight of his life. In their own ways, both were living in a time of dreams.

Browne's dream – a world title bout – was upon him. Adam Saidov, the same child who had sheltered in a cellar, the young student who watched a fighter jet release its rockets at his classroom, the boy who prayed to Allah while huddled in a bathtub, was not seeking glory. His victory, in many ways, had already been won. His triumph lies in the sort of person that he is. It lies in his gentleness, it lies in the love that he had found in his life, it is in the unspoiled way he still views the world and, most of all, it is in his belief in his fellow human beings. Despite the atrocities he witnessed, there is no spite or resentment in him. 'Why would I hate a Russian? That Russian has done nothing to me.'

His humility, empathy and, most certainly, his faith have not been victims of the wars. The tall Chechen, the team's interpreter, the friend and supporter of Lucas Browne, had survived. In Saratov, where his family lived for eleven years, Adam graduated from school with the highest of honours, a gold medal. He then went on to university, choosing the Faculty of International Relations for a simple yet profound reason. 'Since my childhood I wanted to finish war on my native earth.' Again, Adam graduated with a gold medal and the Saidov family was ready to complete its odyssey, returning to their village, Duba-Yurt. That was four years ago.

The family home, like the city of Grozny, was reborn, and Adam's parents live there today. Under that roof also reside Islam and his wife and their young son. Adam's sister, Iman, also married and now has three children with a fourth on the way at the time of writing. Adam, as is befitting in this part of the world that was like the Garden of Eden before the wars, met and married a beautiful young lady named Eve and, together, Adam and Eve are the parents to a much loved and doted-on young daughter. Wife and child live in Duba-Yurt. Every weekend, the extended family gathers at the paternal home and, over a meal, shares the news of the week, just as the generations before them have done.

Adam Saidov works today in Grozny, in the External Relations office of the Chechen government. One of his many tasks is to act as an interpreter for delegations from other countries, be they business, sport or governmental. Along with Ibrahim, he was assigned to be a translator for the team accompanying the Australian challenger to Ruslan Chagaev in Grozny in March 2016. In less than a day, Lucas Browne and Adam Saidov bonded in friendship, these two veterans, one of the ring and the other of war.

Let Adam speak:

Homeland, home, street, close people. For many of my peers, at least outside the republic, it is usual words. But, for me, as well as for thousands of my fellow citizens living in Chechnya, they have got absolutely other sense. I have learned to understand depth of these words and to appreciate that with native land absent, your future is absent. I have learned to look with alarm at the watch if your relatives are late. To look with admiration at the parents, neighbours and just at the people living here in Chechnya who after all the horror and war and ruin, sufferings and losses, haven't forgot to joke, raise children and to believe in good.

CHAPTER FIVE

Back in Sydney's West

I. Grozny Chronicle – Wednesday, 2 March 2016

Today is a crucial day. On a personal level, Lucas's two brothers and a good mate join us, so the band of Aussie believers in downtown Grozny will be complete. I wonder if the band of supporters is growing back home. On a professional level, there is the press conference at 5 pm down on level three of our hotel. For the very first time Lucas Browne and Ruslan Chagaev will be together in the same room.

Over breakfast Philippe informs us that the referee for the fight, Panama's Guillermo Perez Pineda, has withdrawn. His place will be taken by one of the assigned judges, Stanley Christodoulou. The South African will bring a resume to the bout that includes officiating fights involving boxing legends such as Tommy 'Hitman' Hearns, 'Marvelous' Marvin Hagler and the great Roberto Duran. Christodoulou, competent and highly experienced at this elite standard, will bring a degree of calm and control to the fight, his quietly assertive manner ensuring the better fighter on the night has every opportunity for victory. No-one wants a cut caused by a recklessly swinging head to decide the winner of this fight.

The three judges at ringside will be Jean Robert Laine from Monaco, the Thai Pinit Prayadsab and, replacing Christodoulou on the judging bench, from Venezuela, Jesus Cova. We all agree that Lucas has the opportunity to take the decision out of the hands of the three ringside judges, but it is reassuring to have a referee in control who will not be fazed by the anticipated hostile environment inside the Colosseum come this Saturday evening.

The floor ladder and the cups now lie on the carpeted hallway, the session complete. I sit with my back against the wall, legs outstretched, in conversation with Lucas, who sits opposite me, now relaxed and in a mood to talk. He tells me about the improvement that Rodney Williams has brought to his style, the movement, fitness, agility and rhythm. The Lucas Browne that promises to be in the ring against Ruslan Chagaev is certainly the sum of many people's efforts, with the contributions of early mentors cementing his aggressive, 'no prisoners taken' approach.

But there seems to be something unique in this relationship between fighter and trainer. Rodney's quiet approach, his unflappable manner that radiates inner calm, and his emphasis on fundamental skills connect with Lucas at a profound level, bringing out his best. And the changes that have come about are not all physical.

Lucas talks of his battle with the hard-punching Ukrainian Andriy Rudenko in 2014 in Wolverhampton, England. His younger opponent was undefeated and saw the contest as his opportunity to gain a world ranking and a future title shot. Rudenko came into the bout very confident, dismissing Browne's credentials. He claimed he had no fear of fighting a bigger man, even one with the punching power of his Australian opponent and, by rounds six and seven, he may have gone some way to proving his point. Lucas's own mind was just starting to work against him, at least hinting at it, suggesting, 'so this is how you get beaten for the first time'.

While his mind entertained the thought of defeat, his willpower would not. His determination and courage did not desert him when he needed them and, rather than wilt under the pressure that his opponent applied, he rose above it, finding a well of self-belief previously untapped. Browne outboxed Rudenko in the final four rounds to win on points. His preparation for that bout was mediocre; his preparation now for Chagaev is superb.

Like most people, Browne's self-belief and confidence can ebb and flow, sometimes elusive and scarce, at other times present and plentiful. Before me sits a fierce fighter who has metamorphosed into a skilled boxer almost before our eyes. He is a man on a journey, nearing his destination. I spy those cups and rope ladder out of the corner of my eye: his raw power and warrior's spirit are now complemented by light footwork and new combinations. Without them he would not be the contender for the title that he is, just one withering blow on Saturday night away from being the WBA heavyweight world champion.

I think to myself that if Lucas has improved so dramatically in the few short months that Rodney has mentored him, then the sky is the limit. Lucas thinks likewise. The improvement began when Lucas was under the guidance of the great Australian boxer Jeff Fenech, but the chemistry between Lucas and Rodney is something special. It has bred confidence and self-belief in the big man, coming from the knowledge that his trainer has instilled in him new skills and steadily improved his ringcraft.

Like all good trainers and coaches, Rodney is first and foremost a teacher. Yes, he teaches skills and tactics, but it's more than that – he teaches the whole person. Quietly spoken and economical with words, there is no macho bravado and ramped-up hype. He has another characteristic of a good teacher: he does not seek to be the centre of attention; it's all about the student.

Often during these past few days, Rodney could be heard on the phone to his family back home, and Lucas certainly connects with Rodney's love of family. It's a simple thing, but a shared connection like that can bond a student and teacher, establishing the common ground that can be the foundation for the necessary level of trust that makes the relationship work.

Last night, when our Chechen bodyguard Boss Man got into the ring with Rodney, gloves on, ready to hit the pads, was a case in point. Without a single spoken word, using only gestures and eye contact, Rodney quickly turned Boss Man from a brawler who could no doubt win most street fights to a boxer swivelling his hips, transferring his weight, turning his wrist and hitting with genuine power. I looked on, transfixed, not so much by the boxing on display, but by the masterclass of the master teacher before me.

The quality that impresses me most is his calm, inner confidence. It's as if Rodney is the keeper of some *fundamental wisdom or truth and, while his lantern burns, the light will guide and protect, and all will be well. It's quite an aura for a trainer, coach or teacher to possess.*

As we talk, Lucas's mellow R&B music creates a mood of calm before the storm. But it's good old Aussie rock that will echo through the Chechen Colosseum on Saturday night. Lucas has chosen AC/DC's 'Hell's Bells' as the anthem to herald his parade into the ring for his dance with destiny. I can hear it now, the slow, deliberate, apocalyptic chiming of that bell, but it won't be the four horsemen of the End of Days entering the ring, it will be Lucas Browne who will be the harbinger of destruction. At least that's the script that keeps playing out in my mind. From my room I hear fresh Australian accents echoing from Lucas's room and I know that the boys have arrived. Danny, five years older than Lucas, and Patrick, four years his junior, stand with Matt Meyerhoff, Lucas's good mate from Perth and his longtime sponsor and supporter. Spiced with the familiarity of family and friend, good-natured digs and ego-chipping comments bounce back and forth. Their stories of Russian bureaucracy, a night out in Moscow and some messages from home have Lucas as relaxed as he's been since arriving here. The Browne brothers are back together. The lid is off the pressure cooker. Soon enough brotherly banter takes over; boasting takes precedence over a mere world title shot. Danny declares himself the fastest 40-metre sprinter in Grozny and Pat calls his bluff. Tonight they will race in the Akhmat gym: at least one Browne boy will walk away from Grozny with glory.

Our security team has changed shifts, bringing more fresh faces. Boss Man and his two comrades have been replaced by Usman, Khalid and Salman, but Boss Man's team will re-join us on Saturday for the big fight.

Five o'clock is fast approaching and the press conference will bring Lucas face to face with his great opponent for the very first time. I don't know how Lucas feels, but I am excited at the prospect of seeing Chagaev in the flesh. We descend to the third floor of our hotel. To the right is the breakfast area, but we turn left to the press conference room. We arrive ten minutes before the scheduled start and our entire entourage – all ten of us – sit at a table in a far corner of the function room. A long table has been set up under the glare of the TV lights, with seats for the assembled press laid out before it. The only person sitting at the table is Alex Fedesov, the tall, gentlemanly Russian who represents the promotional team and will be hosting the press conference.

To his right are three chairs where the champion's team will sit and to his left are four seats: one for our interpreter, Adam Saidov, who will translate for the benefit of both teams, and three for Lucas's party. As the reporters view the table, from left will sit trainer Pedro Diaz, manager and promoter Timur Dugazaev, the world champion Ruslan Chagaev, Alex Fedesov, Adam Saidov, the challenger Lucas Browne, Philippe Fondu and Matt Clark. For the moment though, only Alex's seat is occupied. Over in our corner of the room, we sit, joke, drink water and wait. And wait. And still we wait.

It is now 5.45 pm, a full forty-five minutes after the scheduled start of the press conference and the general consensus of our team is that the Chagaev team is playing mind games. Always keen to do the right thing, Lucas has *arrived early, but we decide that enough is enough and we wind our way past the press and leave the room to go back to the twenty-fourth floor. If we are going to wait, we will wait in privacy, not like a gang of subservient apprentices awaiting the arrival of the master tradesman.*

We are there only five minutes when Philippe receives the call to inform us that Chagaev's team has now arrived and the conference is about to start. Down we go, retracing our steps, Lucas, Philippe and Matt taking their places at the table under the glare of lights. Alex Fedesov opens the conference by welcoming the journalists, inviting questions from the assembled reporters – and the champion is under the soft spotlight of gentle questioning. The atmosphere is polite and respectful, the tone muted. Chagaev sits back straight, arms folded on the table in front of him, and answers the questions in a quiet voice, looking down in front of him as if gathering his thoughts. I comprehend next to nothing of what Chagaev has to say, not being able to hear Adam's whispered interpretation to Lucas.

On the other hand, I clearly understand Lucas's acknowledgement that Chagaev is experienced and has fought big fights, but points out that he himself is taller, has a great deal of power and has trained to go twelve rounds. When asked the provocative question as to whether he hates his opponent, Lucas answers that he has no reason to do so whatsoever; Chagaev is a family man with a wife and children, just like himself. It may not be the controversial response that the journalist was looking for, but it is typical Lucas Browne, not buying into artificial hype. He sees the pair of them as two warriors, here to do a job, the very same job; one will simply do it better than the other. The press conference is over in about thirty minutes, the teams at the table stand and handshakes are shared.

Lucas Browne and Ruslan Chagaev pose for photos together, standing facing each other, fists cocked, staring menacingly, faces set in aggression. Lucas is clearly bigger than the champion despite the fact that Chagaev wears trainers with raised soles. But the champion is thick-set around the neck, his wide shoulders and upper torso bull-like. Lucas's size and reach advantage promise to be a factor in this fight, but, of course, Chagaev's fast hands and wicked left hook will come to the party as well. Still, we come away from the press conference with our confidence on the rise.

After dinner, our driver, Ruslan, is waiting outside our hotel to drive us out to the Akhmat gym complex. Tonight our party swells by three, with Danny and Pat Browne and Matt Meyerhoff joining us for the first time. The darkened streets are swarming with police and military carrying out their usual duties, hailing down cars, stepping in among lanes of traffic, waving machine guns and searching suspicious vehicles.

Strangely the sight of military in the streets brandishing weapons with implied menace has already lost some of its shock value. Perceiving that we are being afforded special treatment, we can only believe the surveillance, as heavy-handed as it is, is necessary in preventing trouble.

Back in the ring tonight the intensity is back, huge left hooks whistling past Rodney's face and thumping into his hand pad, followed by two rights, the second of which is a thunderclap. How could anyone wear that? It is all business tonight, Rodney sharpening Lucas's preparation like a trainer of a thoroughbred leading into a Melbourne Cup. Lucas looks more focused this evening, lighter on his feet, each jab sharper than yesterday, each right smacking with more ferocity, each combination timed more precisely. Again, his rounded shots are frighteningly heavy. If Lucas is not the biggest hitter in heavyweight boxing, he must be close to it. Tonight I notice more uppercuts being thrown, the punch that could ice a fight when Lucas finds himself close in.

The gym is quiet tonight, the talk between Rodney and Lucas barely audible. The atmosphere is electrically charged, like the air before a storm breaks, an untamed ferocity hovering, threatening to incinerate whatever lies in its path. We are not seeing Chagaev's build-up, so we can only guess about his fitness, preparation and state of mind. What we have seen is the challenger, and you feel that he is building to something very special.

The boxing done, it's time for some track and field. Now that Lucas has completed his workout, he becomes the third Browne brother, a mere bystander to the spectacle that is about to unfold. Danny and Patrick Browne limber up, jogging on the spot, loosening stiff muscles, Pat dressed in rolled-up trousers. The course is agreed upon, up the gym, a touch of the far wall and back to the starting point, close enough to the 40 metres in question. The Brownes take up their starting positions and they are off, tearing down the gym and hitting the far wall almost simultaneously, but Danny has the better technique, his turn is superior to Pat's, and that is where the race is won and lost. Danny has claimed glory and bragging rights. On our way back into downtown

Grozny, the time just past midnight, it seems that we have Tom Hanks in the van with us as Pat perfectly imitates his Southern drawl with quote after quote from Forrest Gump. *Easy laughter fills the bus. You feel another chess piece has been moved strategically into place.*

My journal entry tonight poses two questions. What was the secret of those three or four months when this big-hitting heavyweight joined forces with the understated but shrewd trainer in the sweltering gyms of far western Sydney? And secondly, now that we know that Stanley Christodoulou will control the bout, what will he bring to the contest?

II. The Cake Was Baked

BKH Gym would not be out of place in Philadelphia or the Bronx, deep in the American boxing heartland. With its low ceiling and small-size ring, its shadowy atmosphere oozes struggle and dreams. It's almost as if the walls of the gym have somehow absorbed the sweat and the energy of all those who have trained here. The ghosts of their long-ago efforts still seem to haunt its nooks and crannies.

The BKH gym is on the mezzanine floor of a warehouse in the blue-collar suburb of Kings Park in Sydney's deep west, set in an industrial street full of no-nonsense commercial premises. Many are run-down. The streetscape is all concrete: concreted car parks, wide concrete driveways for heavy trucks, concrete footpaths. Meagre nature strips go untended; weeds struggle between the cracks in the pavement. It's on Tattersall Road, and no doubt many who work here dream of winning the lottery. The primary function of the warehouse is to store concrete formwork and other construction materials produced by the BKH Group. But here, managing director Benny Howlin has found space for one of his passions: boxing.

Just like on the back streets of Philly or the Bronx, a boxing gym in Kings Park can be a most effective classroom for life's hard lessons: 'within these four walls, you get nothing for nothing.' You would guess that most who have stepped inside this gym already know that bottom line.

In the steamy summer months of late 2015 and early 2016, Lucas Browne made the journey here to punch hit-pads, over and over again. It was a hot summer, almost 1.5 degrees hotter than the long-term average – and there sure wasn't any aircon. Drill after drill, hour after hour, day after day, no short cuts, no excuses. He had bought into a plan. This plan had no late-night plotting, no secret schemes, no high-tech identification of an opponent's weakness. This plan was elementary. It was simply about making Browne the most lethal boxer he could be through sheer hard work.

It was late November and Browne had secured the boxer's dream: a title shot. He had recently linked up with local Blacktown trainer Rodney Williams, who had worked in his corner at previous fights. Williams had inherited a fighter with a perfect professional record, one in whom previous trainers Tama Te Huna and Jeff Fenech had fostered aggression and a go-forward style.

An appointment with a world champion looming, Williams did his homework. He sought out footage of just one of Chagaev's previous fights, against British boxer Matt Skelton in January 2008. He identified this particular bout because of the characteristics – and limitations – that Skelton and Browne shared. Skelton, like Browne, was seen as a big puncher, one who went forward looking for his opportunities.

Williams used Skelton's experience against the more refined boxing skills of Chagaev as a teaching tool:

> I watched the Skelton fight. He was pretty much the sort of fighter Lucas was at the time, not much foot or head movement. My message to Lucas was that if you keep doing in the ring what you have been doing, this is what you're going to get from Chagaev. But if you start using evasive movement and working angles in the ring, then you're going to make inroads with him.

Williams' assessment of Browne's style at the time was fairly blunt:

> Your record states that you've been winning fights, but there's no excitement about you. Even if you'd been losing and you looked exciting doing it, you'd be a fighter I'd like to follow. It's head movement, foot movement – they are what make you look exciting as a fighter. Look good, feel good, do good, it all meshes. It's like when a shark gets hold of a sea lion, it doesn't just hold on. Have that sort of feeling about you, look dangerous.

The trainer's impressions were pretty much in line with the thinking of many judges of boxing talent in Australia. Ben Damon, the Main Event fight analyst, was a long-term observer of Browne's development. He summed up his thoughts thus:

> The general consensus of Lucas Browne prior to
> preparing for his world title fight is that he was a big
> puncher, a slow mover and perhaps a one-dimensional
> fighter in that he relied solely on his power. He didn't
> move his feet and he needed to catch you in order to
> stop you.

Ever the realist, Browne listened to Williams and agreed. So Williams went about his task of transforming Browne into a boxer who could move, who could dodge and weave, letting him put his power and reach to greater advantage. Together they worked, rebuilding a technique, remodelling a mindset, refining a toolbox of skills. From the outset, Williams was optimistic about what he had to work with. 'I use drills as diagnostic tools to assess a fighter's ability and athleticism and I was quite impressed with what I saw.'

Along the way, Britain's former world champion Nigel Benn provided his encouragement and assistance in whatever way he could. Browne described the team that now surrounded him:

> I've got the perfect team now and each day I'm
> learning new things. Rodney is the quiet one who
> provides a calming influence and concentrates on the
> pad work – while Nigel is the loud one who shouts
> and gets me pumped up. He's the motivator and the
> cheerleader.

The work for most anyone in Kings Park is hard and repetitious. It was especially so for Browne in that BKH gym during those summer months. Twelve rounds of floor-ladder drills, three minutes each, with a thirty-second break between, followed by a similar session on the hit-pads. Then drills focusing on movement and punching tested his fitness. When it came to fight night in March in Grozny, Browne gave full credit to Williams for pushing him to the limits. 'We covered everything – endurance, cardio, technique. I credit the condition I was in to Rodney.'

Browne explains further:

> Initially we had a chat about what we both wanted and how we would go about it, but all that means nothing until you actually start training and see how you gel. That's when I'd be able to see what his methods are and assess how they might relate to me and my style. After the first session it was an absolute sigh of relief. I had someone who understood what I wanted and someone who wanted to work with what my body could do. I wanted to use my power and my reach and after that first session, I thought that this is going to work.

The repetition was all about muscle memory, one of the trainer's favourite mantras. Browne found himself doing so many footwork drills that his calves cramped. His willpower to fight through the pain became his own private battle, to be fought and won every day of training. But fight it he did, and after four weeks of these mind-numbing drills Browne started to emerge at the other end, a fighter with new skills and a developing bag of tricks. But right to the very end, there were no guarantees.

'It wasn't until the very end of our preparation that I truly believed,' Williams concedes. 'Three weeks out I still had my doubts that he could come out and do what he did. The cake was baked at the last minute.'

III. It's Never About Him

When pressed to identify one repetition that paid dividends in the end, Browne would nominate the cups drill. The same drill he was doing every morning in the hallway of a Grozny hotel: seven or eight cups on the floor in a roughly circular shape, with the fighter required to step quickly between them, balancing on the balls of his feet and switching directions, without upsetting a cup.

He explains the benefit:

> The cups drill made a real difference. It got me moving in and out, going from this angle, turning and going to another angle. You step in, jab and turn away. It was Rod's thing, muscle memory through repetition.

Browne would argue though, that it was the man behind the drills that was more influential than the actual drills themselves. The chemistry between the pair was obvious and palpable: they clicked from the start. All through the challenges of those long, hot months, they were more like a pair of good friends feeding off each other's energy than two professionals contracted to work together. The boxer saw it this way too:

> It wasn't really a fighter–trainer relationship. It was more like two mates talking, just connecting and gelling. We liked the same music, the same style, we'd be dancing in the ring and having a great laugh and it was all actually enjoyable. It was like 'I am going to see Rodney; we'll have a mad old time'.

For his part, the trainer liked what he found in Browne: a desire to improve, an open mind to change and a healthy ego. Williams is a big believer in fighters needing ego and a degree of selfishness to be successful.

'Two things I'll never knock a boxer for are some selfishness and a "they love me" attitude,' Rodney says. 'Some see it as just an oversized ego; I see it as pride. You need it to get the job done in the ring.'

Pride and believing in yourself had been the drum to which Williams marched through life. He was born in 1969, the second of three children, and the oppression of the apartheid system still had a stranglehold on the social structures of Johannesburg, where he was born. As he remembers it, there were three distinct tiers of people, separated by the colour of their skin – and thereby the opportunities that their racial heritage afforded them. He was designated as 'coloured', not as oppressed as those defined as 'black', but certainly not as privileged as those whose skin was deemed to be 'white'.

There were buses, cafes, restaurants and toilets that 'coloured' people were excluded from. Despite the suffocating system, Rodney Williams' dad, Victor, was a computer operator. A shortage of expertise in this area in Australia in the late 1970s provided his family with a chance of a life of more opportunities.

When Victor passed away in Melbourne in 2016, just three weeks after his son took Browne to Grozny, Williams wrote of his dad: 'All that I am and all that I do, I do as this man has shown me through his example.' Fundamental to those life lessons was one that Williams took to heart: 'Always stand up for yourself. Don't let any man or any situation get on top of you.' Williams was grateful that his father had lived to witness the title fight. When the Williams family arrived in Melbourne they had $500 to their name. But they did have a roof over their heads, a home shared with family friends, and Victor had a job waiting for him. He had brought one other thing with him from South Africa: a background in boxing.

Victor Williams had boxed in the gyms around Johannesburg as a boy in the 1950s and fostered an interest in boxing in his son, but drew the line at him stepping into a ring.

So, like many a schoolboy in a similar situation, Rodney Williams funnelled his attention towards those legends of his time – Leonard, Duran, Hagler and Hearns, surnames that require no elaboration, champions from the halcyon days of welterweight and middleweight boxing. Their wars were the backdrop of his youth. He was mesmerised by the silky smooth skills and showman hype of Sugar Ray Leonard, but it was the mighty Marvelous Marvin Hagler who was his favourite. The tough southpaw, with his aggression, punching power and incomparable courage was, for the young Williams, the ultimate fighter. By the time Williams left his family home, with a job to go to, almost the first thing he did was walk into a boxing gym.

Williams was to go on and have twenty-one amateur fights in and around Melbourne, with some success, but by the time he considered turning professional he was already in his mid twenties. His late start in boxing weighed on his mind and the more that he thought about it, the more obvious the way forward seemed. Success was important to him, and it seemed to Williams that his future in boxing was as a trainer, not a boxer.

Just as the finest teachers remember how it feels to be a student, Williams brought the same awareness to training. In his profession, what he recalled clearly was every bout that he ever fought and every training session that he took part in. He believed that taking up training when he did was a blessing – the memory was fresh; he could still feel what his boxers were feeling. Empathy is vital to teaching. He also recognised that he brought an instinctive ability to connect with people. He explains:

> I feel that I'm able to get on the same level as my
> fighters, regardless of age. It's never been something
> I've had to work hard at. It's more a quality I feel I've
> been gifted by the Great Man above. I have an ease with
> communication and in relationships with my boxers.

Browne would recognise these qualities in his trainer and believed that they lifted Williams above the ruck: this ability to understand other people, connect with them, find the secret to unlock their potential, putting their needs first. Browne valued the perceptiveness he found in Williams:

> By me opening up to him and expressing myself, I
> gave him the key to who I am. But, at the same time,
> he provided the scenario for me to do that. It was
> like going to see a 'shrink'; I could talk to him about
> anything and feel comfortable. It's never about him.
> He's never big-noted himself or promoted himself in
> any way. Boxing is his own little niche in life and he
> loves it.

IV. Facing a Southpaw

During the preparation for the world title fight, Team 'Big Daddy' did not place the champion Chagaev under the microscope; there was no intense scrutiny of his style and strengths. Williams was adamant that the result depended more on Browne fighting his game than on a neurotic search for a chink in Chagaev's armour.

What they did focus on however, was the fact that Browne would be facing a southpaw in the ring, and the generic dangers and opportunities that any lefty presents. The plan was simple and twofold. And it all revolved around Browne's favourite weapon, his big right hand.

The first part of the plan depended on footwork. As Chagaev moved forward on his leading right foot, jabbing with his right hand, Browne would look to step outside him with his own left foot. If he managed to dance into that space, it would open a corridor for a straight right from Browne between Chagaev's jab and his left hand glove, straight at an unprotected chin. It was all about body position.

The second tactic involved Browne's trademark punch, his powerful right hook. Fighting a skilful southpaw posed the risk of collecting his power shot, his dangerous left hand, but it also opened up possibilities. If Chagaev were to throw himself into the punch and miss, he would expose the left side of his head to a right-hand counter, and it would be happy days for Lucas Browne.

So the footwork and hit-pad drills were all about body position, working angles and throwing combinations. Like a pair of nimble figure skaters, Williams and Browne glided around the ring together, the fighter throwing ferocious hooks and rips, the trainer catching them in his pads. In a barely audible voice, Williams repeated his gospel over and over again – 'See and react, see and react' – and waved his left pad over Browne's ducking head, miming a Chagaev left hook. Browne did see and did react, responding with a tremendous right hand that his trainer managed to take in his own right pad, centimetres from his left jawline.

As the weeks rolled on, Browne and Williams stepped up the intensity of his sparring sessions, mainly against southpaws, to ready the fighter for what Chagaev would throw at him. The ring in the BKH gym was the ideal size for their purposes. Brown says:

The ring was small, the roof was low. I called it the sweat box. It was just the thing that I needed. When you get into a ring to fight, you're nervous and with all the lights, it's usually hot and humid. The smaller ring size was perfect because it makes the two boxers engage in the sparring session and ensures that you're blocking and guarding.

But, as the summer stretched on, much of the training moved from their cocooned nest at the BKH warehouse over to the Blacktown Police-Citizens Youth Club, where a full-sized ring would now replicate true fight conditions. And a new sparring partner arrived from Marseille, France, another southpaw, the French former heavyweight champion Fabrice Aurieng.

The idea was that Aurieng would provide Browne with sharper and more challenging sessions, readying him for the stern test that loomed in just over a month's time. The Frenchman was seen as an agile boxer in the ring and the belief was that if Browne could go with Aurieng, he'd be able to stick it with Chagaev.

Browne credits the French fighter for helping to put the finishing touches on his fight fitness, but Aurieng took a battering to achieve it. Browne explains:

> I started to work out his style in our first session
> together and, as our spars wore on, I began dropping
> him more and more. Firstly it was my body shots that
> put him on the canvas, then my left hands and finally I
> gave him my rights.

While a fighter preparing for the biggest night of his career would want his sparring partner standing on his feet throwing punches, Browne and his team grew in confidence with each session. Brothers Danny and Pat were regular spectators at his training sessions and, each time Fabrice Aurieng hit the canvas, their belief in their brother's prospects grew. Pat recalls:

> After a few sessions with Fabrice, Lucas started dropping him two or three times a spar. He had to retire a couple of times, saying he just couldn't do it anymore. It's the point where everything Rodney had been teaching Lucas over the past couple of months had become natural habit; good movement, great left body shots. That's when everyone started thinking 'Gee, he's really taken to it, a world title is definitely possible'.

Guiding the preparation of a contender for a world heavyweight title fight would be the highlight of Williams' training career to date. Up for grabs was a unique place in Australian sporting history. But nothing changed with Williams: his tone was just as muted, the drills just as pedantic and the tolerance for short cuts just as short as for any of his boxers. The trainer's quiet, low-key character was just right for Browne. In many ways, it was the sessions that Williams took with lesser athletes than Browne that made him the trainer that he is:

> I have always been grateful to those less gifted fighters that I coach. Top athletes don't teach me anything as a trainer. The ones who teach you the most are the ones with less athletic ability. You try to teach them something as a coach and they just don't get it, so you try another way of teaching the same thing and it's

still lost on them. You try a third way of explaining it and by the time you've got the message across, you the teacher have learned three ways of expressing the very same skill.

Even if Williams hadn't learned a great deal from the fine athlete that was Lucas Browne, he had helped to facilitate the change in style that both thought necessary. With a new repertoire of combinations, a sharper jab, lightness on his feet and a willingness to work angles, Lucas 'Big Daddy' Browne was primed and ready to rip in.

Maybe a true metamorphosis had taken place over the months sweating it out in the BKH and Blacktown gyms. Maybe an all-round multiskilled boxer had emerged from a one-dimensional slugger. Would it be enough to lift a piece of the fragmented world heavyweight title? Maybe, but one thing was certain: the fighter that Chagaev would meet in the ring in Grozny would not be the fighter he had been expecting. Williams was sure of that. And Browne knew he had more weapons in his arsenal than ever before.

Yet Browne was more aware than anyone that a knockout in Grozny would take the judges' scorecards out of the equation. It was all down to him, Chagaev and the third man in the ring, the referee. He did not know it yet, but that man would be Stanley Christodoulou.

V. The Third Man in the Ring

In December 1973 American light-heavyweight Bob Foster stepped into the ring in Rand Stadium, Johannesburg, to defend his world title against the South African Pierre Fourie. The pair had met previously; only months before, Foster had retained his crown with a dominant display in New Mexico. But, in their second contest, the two fighters were to make South African history.

When Foster, an African-American, stood in that ring facing Fourie, it was the very first time a black man and a white man would fight in a South African professional boxing ring. That aspect of the event, just as much as the event itself, was huge news in South Africa and a multiracial audience of more than 35,000 fans filled the stadium.

For the fight to even take place Prime Minister B.J. Vorster had to amend the *Boxing and Wrestling Control Act* that prohibited interracial fights in those years controlled by apartheid. It would be another twenty-one years before the system was overturned and state-controlled racial segregation would end.

Again Bob Foster took the prize, but, more importantly, by just being in the ring with Fourie, he played his role in forming the South African sporting landscape of the years to come.

Sometimes the seeds for sweeping social change are cultivated on the grand stage of a world title bout, sometimes on the parliamentary benches, but, critically, those seeds are often sown on the back pages of history, by the coalface workers, by those not seeking recognition, but with hearts fired by passion for what they do.

Stanley Christodoulou was at the coalface then and in the years leading up to that historic fight. From the age of seventeen, armed with the permit required by a white man to visit a black township in those days, Christodoulou had been officiating at boxing nights in the struggling communities, encouraging their development, providing pathways for their boxers, building bridges of hope and acceptance. At one stage he attended fifty-four consecutive official tournaments in the Transvaal Province, his only reward being the satisfaction and experience of promoting boxing among the people of those regions.

When Bob Foster touched gloves with Pierre Fourie, Christodoulou was executive director of the South African Boxing Commission and remembers that moment in time – and its ramifications – fondly:

> Professional boxing in this country led the way to sporting integration. I was very proud to see that fight happen. It showed that in a boxing ring, we could whup each other, irrespective of race, colour or creed.

Today, living in the secluded, idyllic Prince's Grant on the Indian Ocean seaboard just north of Durban, Stanley Christodoulou is quite literally a living legend of the sport. His list of achievements and honours is staggering: he is a member of the International Boxing Hall of Fame, he has refereed or judged an unprecedented total of 235 world title fights, in forty-two countries across six continents; he was the first man to referee and then also judge title fights in seventeen weight divisions; he has received awards from the highest-profile dignitaries on the planet and he has rubbed shoulders with the giants of the sport.

He has twice been named South African boxing's Man of the Year and the WBA honoured him as its Referee of the

Year in 1980. On top of these honours, he has served as the executive director of his nation's Boxing Board of Control and is a very active member of the WBA's International Officials Committee. Quite a resume. But it doesn't end there.

He best tells it himself:

> I had gained a reputation amongst the township
> communities for the work I had done with them over
> the years and when President Mandela came to power,
> I was honoured not just once, but twice for the role
> I had played. And then when the queen came to visit
> our country, the president invited me to a function as a
> guest. I was very honoured because he was such a big
> boxing man. He knew about my career because of the
> different things I was doing in various areas to help
> promote boxing.

But perhaps Christodoulou's greatest achievement lies in being the dignified gentleman that he is, the unaffected manner in which he speaks of himself, the fact that he still looks outward, to where others may need him. He is still spreading the gospel and taking his skills to many disadvantaged corners of the globe. He has delivered workshops and programs in countries such as Namibia, Kenya, Uganda and India, training officials and developing boxing boards to oversee the sport's growth. At seventy years of age, he is very much a fit, energetic man, one with the fire still burning. That fire was lit many years before when growing up in the tough working class suburb of Brixton, in Johannesburg. For a boy of Cypriot heritage in the 1950s, you had to either stand up for yourself in the backstreets of Brixton or be a victim. For a boy born and bred in South Africa, being denigrated and called a foreigner by some of the hard-headed Afrikaner lads in his neighbourhood was simply unacceptable. So Stanley Christodoulou fought back. He recalls those far-away days clearly.

'Fighting back was a means of survival. I wouldn't take it lying down so I learned to use my fists and beat them in a street fight.'

As fortune would have it, there was a boxing gym opposite the grocery store run by the Christodoulou family and that is where his love affair with boxing started.

Christodoulou won all twelve of his amateur fights, but never really rated his own style, his street-fighting ways winning out over boxing finesse. But it would be as third man in the ring – or judging the contest – that Christodoulou would discover his niche in the sport. Not long out of school, he was working at a branch of Barclays Bank when a client who was instantly recognisable to the avid boxing fan strode in one day. The customer was Willie Toweel, an accomplished member of the famous South African boxing family. The two struck up a friendship and it was Toweel who started the younger Christodoulou's education in officiating fights, escorting him out to the black townships to judge tournaments.

Christodoulou's career blossomed from there. In 1973 he refereed his first world title bout, and what a fight to cut your teeth on. South Africa's Arnold Taylor met the Mexican Romeo Anaya in what would be considered one of the top bantamweight title fights of all time. The referee recalls it this way:

It was one of the most brutal fights you could ever
see. Both fighters were knocked down and both were
cut. Taylor was down four times before he floored the
champion in the fourteenth round. I was very proud to
be involved in that event.

As dramatic as that particular fight was, if there was
one landmark battle that the referee would be known for,
it would be the Marvin Hagler showdown with Roberto
Duran at Caesar's Palace in Las Vegas. It was November
1983 and the pair of boxing greats faced off for Hagler's
middleweight crown.

For much of that classic contest the Panamanian held his
own, dominating two of the three scorecards after thirteen
rounds. But Hagler came home the stronger to take those
final two rounds and the fight.

Going into the clash, Hagler's camp had drawn attention
to Duran's style of fighting, which some saw as dirty, so the
spotlight was always going to be on how Christodoulou
controlled the fight. As it would turn out, the referee was
always in control while still letting the contest flow.

Christodoulou remembers Duran's reputation, but also
the deep respect that he has always held for the Panamanian
boxer.

Duran had quite a reputation for being a dirty fighter
and, in the second or third round of that fight, he
landed a low blow. I said 'Stop. Keep your punches up',
and immediately I got his attention. It was one of the
easiest fights to referee because he obeyed the rules and

followed my directions. Roberto Duran was a great
fighter and had the respect of the other boxers.

Christodoulou's career would see him referee or judge
fights involving Tommy Hearns, Emile Griffith, Victor
Galindez, the Australian Johnny Famechon, Aaron Pryor,
Lennox Lewis, Evander Holyfield and, soon, Ruslan Chagaev
and Lucas Browne.

In 1976 Christodoulou attended the WBA's World
Convention in Washington DC and came away from it with
perhaps the most prized possession of his life.

While at the convention he met arguably the two greatest
heavyweights of all time, Muhammad Ali and Joe Louis.
'Muhammad Ali was outstanding in every respect. And
Joe Louis, he was simply a great person. I admired him so
much. It was an honour to meet them.' Forty years later,
Christodoulou still treasures the photograph taken at that
convention. It shows the WBA official, the one with the
tough street fighter from Brixton somewhere still inside him,
standing between the two legends, Ali and Louis.

The fight game has been a lifelong passion for Stanley
Christodoulou, one that shows no sign of slackening. As
he puts it himself: 'When boxing gets into your blood, it's
addictive.'

In March 2016 he would travel to Grozny to judge the
WBA world title fight between Ruslan Chagaev and Lucas
Browne. In the days before the bout, the South African would
be upgraded to be the third man in the ring. The fighters
could not have been in better hands.

CHAPTER SIX

The Fight Looms

I. Grozny Chronicle – Thursday, 3 March 2016

Just two days to go. Grozny City Hotel is getting busier as boxers, their parties and guests arrive for the big night. The foyer that only yesterday was quiet and empty is now bustling with suitcases and gym bags, buzzing with African languages and Eastern European accents. A big-event atmosphere is upon us; gone is the quiet solitude of the past few days, replaced by TV crews, organisers and support teams.

The scene is electric at breakfast, the sedate, laid-back mood of previous mornings replaced by an almost contagious excitement. If the public areas of the hotel had seemed like our turf previously, they are suddenly owned by the event. It's harder to find a table and to order my flat white from the barista. I don't sit close to Lucas this morning. I'm feeling poorly, suffering from a headache and sore throat. How would it be if I gave a dose of the flu to the challenger two days before the biggest fight of his career? No, it's better I keep my distance, so I share breakfast with our Chechen guards.

Random events, experiences and feelings dominate my thoughts. Our chant of 'Siylah Boss Man', a Chechen term we have learned meaning 'Boss Man the great', when a security officer tries to tell him he can't park directly outside a shopping centre and just cops a dismissive spray in return. Rodney mumbling inside the ring 'The first pay day I'll get from him and I'll be paying for an elbow operation', so hard is Lucas thumping the hit-pads on his trainer's hands. Being welcomed warmly and sincerely by the Muslim people with 'Salaam aleikum' – 'peace be upon you' and us responding 'Aleikum salaam' – 'and upon you the peace'.

The respectful humility of the people, from those in the street, who request photos with Lucas, to retired Olympians and champion fighters such as Uzbekistan's Muhammad Abdullaev. Then there is the enigmatic little Chechen who walks the treadmill in his slippers, a towel covering the dials of the machine, mobile phone constantly at his ear and the occasional Tourette-like outburst of 'arrrgh'. It has become our war cry. It would be true to say that we all came to Grozny with a little apprehension – and we will all leave Grozny with some affection and appreciation.

Just before lunch, Brian Minto joins us in Grozny. He is a former top-shelf contender from Pennsylvania, but at forty-one is looking for a decent payday from a fight he has taken at very short notice. After twenty hours of flying, he is looking very jet-lagged. I take him up to the restaurant on the top floor for some food. In between yawns, he tells me about his misgivings in coming to a country like Chechnya. He has the flags of the US and Ukraine, expressing his pride in his family heritage, tattooed on his back and is concerned how the

Chechen crowd will respond to them. Brian is a heavyweight fighting in a cruiserweight's body and on Saturday night will face the rangy young German boxer Edmund 'Vlad' Gerber directly before Lucas's world title shot; quite a task for a man not long off an international flight.

Soon it is lunchtime and we are joined upstairs by Lucas and the rest of the team. We sit at the long wooden tables, the glass-topped dome of our restaurant acting as a greenhouse, trapping the warmth of the day. Warmer still is the conversation and the mood. Lucas kicks back, scanning social media or talking with his children back home.

Earlier, he was more earnest. He spoke of his father, who died in his backyard, in Baulkham Hills, near his pigeon pen, a place he loved. A heart attack struck him down aged 56. As Browne tells me this, I can't help but notice the tear tattoo under his eye.

Danny now talks about his dad, how he hasn't gotten over losing him. Only days earlier he had promised to accompany Danny to the greyhound races to watch one of his dogs compete, but fate intervened. Friends convinced Danny to still go: 'It's what your dad would want.' In the running, the dog was not rated a chance, but, of course, it somehow got home. I become aware of the piped music, humming softly in the background. I know it's been playing constantly at every meal, but it's been dinner music, uninspiring and soporific. Now my ears tune in, way before anyone else detects the significance. Or is it just me and my era? Perhaps I am the only one in Team 'Big Daddy' who knows and loves the Simon and Garfunkel composition 'The Boxer'. Rather than an uplifting message to the boxer like 'Eye of the Tiger' in the Rocky movies, *this song would be more suited to the soundtrack of* Requiem for a Heavyweight *or* Million Dollar Baby, *a lament for a fighter who has been chewed up and discarded. Not quite the song for Lucas's entrance to the ring on Saturday night, but nevertheless, it serves its purpose for me.*

I have a sense that the song is an omen heralding the advance of something monumental and life-changing, something gathering energy and growing, a thing that both promises and threatens, blowing in from afar.

With Lucas having an afternoon rest, Matt and I want to return to the markets, and we take a nervous Brian Minto with us. As we snake our way through the stalls and tight alleyways, I hear Brian behind me mumbling in his Yankee accent 'Oh man.' But all is well. Some of the merchants recognise us as being in Lucas's team and we are treated like royalty, again posing for photos and shaking hands.

It is obvious that Lucas's presence in the streets of Grozny has struck a chord with these people. Maybe it's because he has been there, visible among them, while their champion is secreted away, living in the president's fortified palace. Some merchants whisper 'In my heart I go for Lucas Browne', but then place their index finger to their pursed lips, indicating that it is our little secret.

But I don't think there will be too many fans at the Colosseum Sports Hall in two days' time cheering for Lucas. The thought makes me realise what a lonely sport boxing is. Has any Australian boxer gone as far into the den of the lion as Lucas has here? I don't believe so, especially when you consider that the champion he will face in the ring may not be his biggest threat. And I still have this nagging question about why the Australian media coverage of him is lukewarm and lacklustre. They don't believe he can win. I think to myself as we walk back to our hotel that there are many boxing fans back home who know he can do this. Admittedly a few media pundits think likewise. We here have the best view – and we believe he can win. It's 8 pm and we catch the lifts downstairs where Ruslan is waiting with the van for our journey out to the Akhmat gym. Two variables from our normal routine tonight: Brian Minto has joined us in the van and the workout tonight will be a session open to the press. The quiet solitude of the gym last evening is sure to be displaced by the excitement of cameras, reporters and onlookers. This will be the first opportunity for the Chechens and, for that matter, Chagaev's camp to see something of what Lucas will bring to the table. I doubt that Lucas and Rodney plan to go full throttle and reveal too much, but still, this is their one and only ring session today, and in all likelihood the last before the fight, so they will want to use it well.

We have been informed that Chagaev has been scheduled for his session at 7 pm, so we anticipate that he will be finished and gone when we arrive closer to 9 pm. In keeping with the philosophy that started back in the BKH gym in Kings Park, we are not intent on spying on Lucas's opponent.

When our van pulls in at the gates of the gym's compound, the atmosphere has changed dramatically. Gone is the indifferent shrug of the guard's shoulders to permit our entry into the fortified area. Instead, we encounter beefed-up security, in numerical terms as well as in the weapons that some are carrying.

One guard scans our van, holding a grenade-launcher, while others are clearly alert and ready for anything. Something different is in the air tonight. We are delayed while Adam chats with the guards, who eventually permit our entry. We drive a further 300 metres, where we encounter the second checkpoint. Here security is just as tight, the weapons just as threatening. Again Adam negotiates our entry to the inner section of the compound, and our van traces its way slowly along the driveway. Military guards lurk in the semi-darkness, keepers of the watch.

In the foyer to the gym there are many more pairs of shoes than usual, neatly lying there waiting for their owners' return. We walk into the main gym. There, sitting on a stool next to the ring, is none other than the President of the Chechen Republic, Ramzan Kadyrov, the hardened war veteran, the iron fist that wields absolute power in a once lawless country. The WBA world champion Ruslan Chagaev stands nearby, but it is the president whose hands are being wrapped for the ring. He looks over at us, head tilted forwards, his steady gaze challenging the intruders. So we see that President Kadyrov is preparing to take to the ring himself while Chagaev delays. It seems that Lucas's schedule must once again bow to the routine of the champion.

Lucas takes it all in his stride and retreats to the far side of the gym, sitting on the gym mat, back against the wall. His two brothers and Rodney take up position with him, coolly waiting for events to take their course.

The rest of us drift back over to the cage-fighting ring into which the president has now entered. He has gloved up and is prancing around, shadow-boxing, warming up for who *knows what. Soon a young fighter moves past us and the fifty or so Chechens who have gathered around. He enters the ring with his president.*

Kadyrov is soon moving, jabbing and hooking, timing some of his punches with power and precision. Anyone who knows anything about this man is aware that he can box: we've all seen footage of him sparring with Chagaev. Yet you can't help but wonder how hard his young opponent is trying, for I don't see him land a blow on his opponent. As Kadyrov throws a combination, he yells something in Chechen that draws laughter from his audience. He is the focus of all attention.

Finally the president concedes the spotlight to the champion. Maybe he sees that Chagaev is ready to take to his work or maybe Chagaev has tactfully waited for his president to tire; whichever it is, Kadyrov exits the cage-fighting ring while the champion enters the boxing ring. He completes a very light session on the pads with his trainer, Pedro Diaz, quick jabs and looking sharp enough, but maybe a little pudgy around the midriff.

The champion's session is only ten minutes in when there are three in the ring, as President Kadyrov joins Chagaev and Diaz, boosting their energy, bellowing loudly, seemingly giving his own advice to the boxer. The Chechen leader obviously has a deep respect for the warrior that Ruslan Chagaev is, but to an outsider the champion seems a little like a prized thoroughbred that the president pampers and protects, but, above all else, owns. What will he do if the unthinkable occurs? Will he discard his coveted possession if Lucas breaks it? We shall see. For now Lucas is cool and unfazed.

After his session Chagaev gives a short press interview, noticeably blowing a little from his work-out. The president stays. With bodyguards hovering in the background, he mixes with the crowd milling around the gym adjacent to the ring that the champion has just vacated. Legs apart and arms folded across his chest, he is in relaxed conversation with his people. We Australians seize the chance that has presented itself. All seven of us pose with President Kadyrov for photos, mobile phones being passed back and forth for this once-in-a-lifetime opportunity. He is very patient with us, shaking our hands, the ultimate gracious host.

But the president has not completed his exercise for the night. What sparks him off is lost in translation for us, but once again, President Ramzan Kadyrov is stepping and shadow-boxing, this time on the gym floor outside the ring. The crowd gathers round, forming a circle surrounding him. Fascinated by the unusual spectacle before us, we all join the circle, Lucas standing directly to my right.

The president enjoys the moment, jabbing and hooking at his invisible opponent, the crowd indulging him with laughter and applause. This seems to be where he thrives, in the spotlight of attention.

Then, the unbelievable happens. As the president shuffles around the imaginary ring, he approaches the spot where Lucas stands – and suddenly makes a lunge towards him, fist cocked. Surely this is a pantomime; the president will feint and move away, smug in the drama he creates. But no, he doesn't feint. He doesn't hold the punch – he delivers it. Lucas 'Big Daddy' Browne, the contender for a world title in just two days' time, is punched in the stomach by the President of the Chechen Republic, Ramzan Kadyrov.

Perhaps it is just bravado, a masculine gesture of respect between two warriors, one a boxer and the other a combat veteran, but it remains what we just saw: the president punched Lucas. Not with violent force, but hard enough when Lucas is not expecting it, though he does not give the president the satisfaction of flinching. Still, he is stunned, scarcely believing what just took place.

The Chechen leader has had enough for the moment and the circle breaks up, the group of onlookers doing likewise, many now departing the gym, not at all interested in what the challenger has to offer.

President Kadyrov remains and turns his attention to the ring when Lucas and Rodney climb through the ropes.

The president climbs up onto the canvas and leans against the ropes, alone on his side of the ring apron, directly opposite Matt and I. Rodney leads Lucas through some very light warm-up drills, gently tapping the hit-pads with short uppercuts thrown in quick succession. Kadyrov imitates Lucas, referring to the lack of firepower on show. Rather than mockery, his banter seems good-natured. Lucas and Rodney laugh along with him.

Soon enough, Lucas warms to his task and those familiar thudding left rips and right hooks start exploding into the pads. Certainly Lucas is working harder than Chagaev did and maybe, via the press and, more directly, through the president, he is sending a clear, unequivocal message to Chagaev and his camp that the sternest of challenges awaits. However, the president intimates that it is the hit-pads and not Lucas's power that is producing the intimidating thunder, but you feel that he knows better.

During a break in the session, Rodney comments to President Kadyrov that he wished that we in Australia had a leader who loved the sport of boxing as much as he obviously does and, through Adam's translation, thanks him for the way that our team has been received in Grozny, humbled as we are by the warm welcome of the Chechen people. The president smiles and nods his head in acknowledgement and the Chechens gathered around the ring applaud in response. Rodney has a way of capturing the moment with grace and diplomacy.

When the president and his countrymen have departed we once again have the gym to ourselves. Lucas has completed his work and we chew over the events of the evening.

Beyond appraisal of the champion's and challenger's sessions, the topic of conversation is Lucas being struck by the president. Where else in the world would the head of government be in a boxing ring, let alone throwing a punch, however innocuous, at a boxer about to contest for the world heavyweight title? Probably because of the importance of tonight's activity and the presence of the Chechen president, Shamil has re-joined the bodyguard team this evening. So Lucas takes the man in charge of his security to task, glaring at him, and, with his tongue firmly in his cheek, demands to know where he was the very first time that he needed him. With a smile, Boss Man replies through Adam's translation. 'If that man hits you once, then I will hit you twice.'

At least we know for certain where Boss Man's true loyalties lie.

Our van traces its way home along the highway, headlights penetrating the darkness of the post-midnight Chechen landscape, through Grozny's neighbouring city of Argun, past the congregating militia, around the roundabout and its enormous globe of the world with the twin Shaky Isles, into the outskirts of the capital and, finally, into the city centre and our hotel.

All the way, the Browne brothers belt out pitch-perfect songs. When they break into Extreme's 'More Than Words', their three voices, like a sorcerer's wand, weave their own harmonic magic and everyone else is silenced. You feel they have sung together many times before; that there have been many rehearsals for this rendition in the back of a VIP bus in Grozny. Today has been a key day in the preparation for the fight. The challenger has come face to face with the champion and I consider how they compare. What record does each bring to the title fight? If I were to wipe away all the emotion, wishful thinking and blind optimism, what would be left of Lucas's chance of toppling the reigning champion? That's the question my journal poses to me tonight. Can Lucas Browne beat Ruslan Chagaev?

II. Smokin' Joe Versus Big George

Lucas Browne, all 196 centimetres and 115 kilograms of him, is thirty-six years of age, in the mid ages for a heavyweight fighter, a time when most have well and truly matured, cashed in on their ability and peeked down the other side of the hill towards inevitable decline. But in Lucas's case, he is fresh of mind and body, only twenty-three bouts into his professional career and still developing his skills.

Ruslan Chagaev measures 180 centimetres and usually weighs in at just under Browne's weight. He is a year older and his thirty-seven professional fights were preceded by a lengthy amateur stint. Chagaev will bring the guaranteed class to their fight; Browne will bring the enthusiasm and sense of opportunity. There is a case to be made that the champion has already peaked, that his reflexes have slowed marginally, that he is not quite the razor-sharp puncher that he once was. Nevertheless, he has won his last seven title fights.

Chagaev and Browne are opposites in many ways. Chagaev, the quietly spoken Uzbek, commenced his professional boxing career with a long, distinguished amateur record, including two stunning victories over the legendary Cuban Felix Savon. When he entered the professional ranks, he had a wealth of experience to draw upon. On the other hand, the first boxing bout of the tall, outgoing Australian was also his first professional bout, against countryman Jason Kier on 20 March 2009. He learned his craft on the run, in the ring. Before that, he had had one fight in the cage of mixed martial arts, and for a while he fought concurrently in both rings – hardly a conventional platform from which to launch the career of Australia's best-performed heavyweight of all time.

In the ring in Grozny on 5 March 2016, the Chechen audience and boxing fans watching around the world would see in the blue corner the challenger from Sydney, Australia, with a perfect record of twenty-three fights, twenty-three victories, twenty of them knockouts. In the red corner was the two-time world champion, originally from Uzbekistan, now the adopted son of Chechnya, with thirty-seven professional bouts for thirty-four wins, two defeats and one draw.

Physically, what they would see were two quite different men. The outgoing nature of the challenger seemed to be extended to his appearance, head shaved, heavily tattooed on his back, chest, arms and neck, his country's flag emblazoned on his trunks. The champion, dressed in his trademark black, and his full head of hair and thick beard, appeared equally intimidating, but in a more sullen, unspoken kind of way. He also wore his nation's flag into the ring, his draped across his shoulders, to be respectfully removed for the business to begin.

A boxing historian could see similarities to the 1970s match-up between Joe Frazier and George Foreman. Frazier was not a southpaw like Chagaev, but stood the same 180 centimetres, giving a distinct height advantage to Foreman, just as Chagaev does to Browne. The Australian challenger enjoys a sizeable reach advantage over the champion, again just as Foreman did against Smokin' Joe. And in the ring Chagaev, while not always rolling forward like Frazier, is often the hunter, brooding, crouched, always moving and swaying, seeking weaknesses and never giving his quarry a moment's peace. Browne, though he came into this fight with the reputation for being less agile and light-footed than Foreman, had one major common trait – the heaviest punch in the business.

On 22 January 1973 'Big' George Foreman used that superior punching power to devastating effect. He entered the ring in Kingston, Jamaica, to face the reigning WBA and WBC world heavyweight champion Joe Frazier, both undefeated in their professional careers. Foreman attacked Frazier with vicious hooks and uppercuts, sending him to the canvas three times in that stunning first round. When the bell rang, the champion found himself climbing up off the canvas. The second round offered no respite, with Foreman having zeroed in on his now gravely damaged target. Frazier went down and bravely staggered up three more times before referee Arthur Mercante called an end to the mugging. The previously indestructible champion, the conqueror of 'The Greatest', Muhammad Ali, had just been bashed and thoroughly dismantled by Foreman's heavy artillery. When the pair met for a rematch in New York on 15 June 1976, Ali had spoiled both of their records. Ali had taken Foreman's world crown in the Rumble in the Jungle in Zaire in 1974 and had twice inflicted losses on Frazier in a pair of gruelling wars of attrition.

At that rematch in Uniondale, New York State, in June 1976, Frazier was intent on avoiding early decimation from the big bombs he now knew could bring him disaster. The power puncher forced the aggressor to change his fight plan. It didn't work. Frazier's defensive work kept him out of trouble in the early rounds, but, in the fifth, a huge left hook found the sweet spot and Frazier went down. In the sixth, Frazier's trainer, Eddie Futch, stepped into the ring to call an end to proceedings.

That was nearly forty years ago, and neither Chagaev nor Browne could claim the legendary quality of that pair of warriors, but the similarities of physiques, style and strengths between the combatants raised interesting parallels. Of course, fights from the past are just that – history, filed away in memory, books, videos and dusty newspaper archives. Boxing history is effective in shaping future results only as much as a fighter's mind will permit it to. The one absolute fact coming from this comparison is that Browne could see his similarities to Foreman. He was to go into the fight with Chagaev with the awareness that he possessed arguably the heaviest punch in the division. But that would amount to nothing if he were unable to land it.

III. Beating Felix Savon

Chagaev had suffered defeat only twice in his professional career, once to the clinical reigning world champion, the Ukrainian Wladimir Klitschko, and once to the Olympic gold medallist and one time WBA regular heavyweight world champion, the Russian Alexander Povetkin. He had never been knocked out. Browne was undefeated in his professional boxing career, but had certainly never stepped into the ring with the quality of fighter that Chagaev had mixed it with. No Klitschkos, Povetkins or Oquendos. His biggest-name opponents were Rudenko, Towers and Toney. A vastly experienced world champion from Uzbekistan matched up against an Australian challenger, much the same age, but with quite a different pathway to the door of the Colosseum Sports Hall.

Chagaev is associated mostly with Chechnya by the boxing public, having been sponsored and adopted by President Kadyrov. However, Chagaev was born in the ancient city of Andijan in Uzbekistan's fertile Fergana Valley, with its warm summers and snow-bound winters. He grew up there, launched his amateur career there and fights under its flag. At the 1997 World Amateur Championships in Budapest, Hungary, the great Felix Savon, with two Olympic gold medals and the previous five amateur World Championships, was fighting for a sixth – against Chagaev, who had just turned nineteen.

But the quick hand speed and the stinging left that would become Chagaev's trademark were already present and he scored an upset decisive points victory over Savon. Chagaev was the gold medal winner as a heavyweight at the World Championships; but only for a short time.

When he stepped into the ring in Budapest, Chagaev already had two professional fights to his name. He had travelled to Illinois in the United States and, in the space of a fortnight in August and September 1997, just seven weeks before the World Amateur Championships, fought two American journeymen in a professional ring. He knocked them both out. But, along the way, he knocked himself out of the amateur championships. When his incursion into professionalism was discovered, his gold medal victory over Savon was overturned and the Cuban was awarded the title.

Chagaev would be soon readmitted to the amateur ranks when his bouts in America were declared exhibition fights. But the fact remained that in the ring Chagaev had prevailed over Savon. Chagaev scored a repeat victory over Savon in the final of an international boxing cup in Bulgaria in 1999. And in 2001 he would take the amateur heavyweight title – and this time he would keep it. The future WBA champion finished the amateur phase of his boxing journey with three Asian Games gold medals, one World Championship gold medal, having contested two Olympics. Browne, by comparison, had no amateur record at all.

IV. A Two-Time World Champion

It was in the United States that Chagaev launched his professional career, with six of his first seven fights contested on American shores. After that Chagaev would not fight outside Europe again. He was now living in Hamburg, Germany, and most of his fights would be staged there. One such bout was in Dusseldorf, November 2006, when he fought former two-time heavyweight champion John Ruiz for the right to fight for the title. He got through. Waiting for him was the hulking Russian giant Nikolai Valuev. Chagaev prevailed in a fight where the ascendancy swayed back and forth. The challenger for the WBA world title stood a full 33 centimetres shorter than the champion, who measured a colossal 213 centimetres. Possibly even more concerning was the reach advantage enjoyed by the Russian, 28 centimetres, ideally suiting his major weapon, his snapping jab. So they lined up together in Stuttgart in April 2007, Valuev's world title belt on the line.

Chagaev was twenty-eight years old, loaded with defensive know-how. He went into the bout with a clear plan to use those defensive skills and his agility to take the Russian's size advantage out of the equation. And it worked.

He proved an elusive target for the big man, mobile and bobbing, his head and torso moving to avoid Valuev's big jabs. When on the attack, Chagaev found his range, often scoring with his clinical left hand, which had surprising power behind it at times. The judges scored it 115–113, 114–114 and 117–111. The Uzbek had become the first Asian boxer to claim a heavyweight world title.

The new champion went on to successfully defend his title against Matt Skelton – the one fight of his that Team 'Big Daddy' had analysed. A rematch with Valuev was set up. Then disaster struck. In his very last sparring session before the fight, Chagaev sustained a complete tear of an Achilles tendon, ruling him out of the showdown. The World Boxing Association had little choice but to declare Chagaev 'champion in recess', sanctioning Valuev and Ruiz to meet for his cherished crown. It would be thirteen months between fights for Chagaev. The waters around Chagaev and the World Boxing Association world heavyweight title were now muddied indeed. He was to meet the Costa Rican boxer Carl Davis Drumond as the 'champion in recess', while the man he had earlier conquered, Nikolai Valuev, was recognised as the regular champion after disposing of John Ruiz in August 2008.

Drama seemed to be a close travelling companion of Chagaev at the time. He scored a technical decision victory over Drumond after he sustained a cut to his left eye from two accidental head clashes in the early rounds. With the blood flow hampering his vision, the referee stopped the fight in the sixth round. The decision went to Chagaev with all three judges having him winning the fight at that point.

The pathway to tidying up the titles mess now lay open. The WBA mandated that Valuev and Chagaev would meet for a second time, scheduled for 30 May 2009.

But that fight was never to happen. What Chagaev's camp signed up for was a shot at Wladimir Klitschko, the great Ukrainian champion, the holder of the IBF, WBO and IBO world titles. Having failed to meet his commitment to face Valuev, the WBA moved against Chagaev in July 2009, withdrawing his 'champion in recess' title. Before that happened, however, Klitschko would hand Chagaev his first professional defeat. Towering over his opponent and with a significantly longer reach, Klitschko completely dominated the fight and dictated its rhythm. He clinically took Chagaev apart, constantly flicking out that stinging jab and cashing in with heavier crosses that stunned the Uzbek. Eventually, Chagaev cracked under the unrelenting pressure and was unable to answer the bell for the tenth round.

His loss was to a man who would go on to be the second-longest reigning world heavyweight champion ever, with only the immortal Joe Louis ahead of him. Further, Klitschko would have twenty-three successful defences of his title, again second only to the 'Brown Bomber'. There was little shame to be found in defeat to Wladimir Klitschko.

Klitschko would add the WBA world title to his list of accomplishments when he defeated Britain's David Haye. The World Boxing Association responded by declaring the Ukrainian the super champion of the world, again opening an opportunity for Chagaev to snatch back his regular title belt.

In August 2011 he lined up against the undefeated Russian Alexander Povetkin, the gold medal winner from the Athens Olympics. The pair put on a stoush that night in Erfurt, Germany, with willing exchanges in a fight that ebbed and flowed. Povetkin outjabbed Chagaev early, but in the middle rounds Chagaev's trademark crunching lefts found their range and he had his opponent stunned and retreating.

But Povetkin held his nerve and came back at Chagaev strongly in the closing rounds to take a close, but unanimous, victory. When Chagaev met Browne in Grozny in 2016, these two losses to Klitschko and Povetkin were his only defeats. Before Browne, though, Chagaev would win back the WBA regular world title. He won his next five fights following the Povetkin loss and, in July 2014, met the experienced American Fres Oquendo for the vacant title. By now Chagaev was under the guidance of astute trainer Pedro Diaz. Known as the 'boxing professor', the Cuban took over Chagaev's preparation following the unexpected passing of his previous trainer and good friend, Fritz Sdunek.

Oquendo didn't turn up in Grozny until the day before the fight, hardly an ideal preparation. The bout itself was lacklustre, but resulted in Chagaev scoring a close points win. The Uzbek was now a two-time world champion.

In July 2015, Chagaev defended his title against Francesco Pianeta in Germany, winning in the first round. The WBA regular champion now awaited a fight against the rising, but still low-profile Australian, Lucas Browne. What would he bring to the table?

V. A Big Right Hand

At much the same time as Chagaev was in the German city of Rostock on the Baltic Sea coastline preparing for his comeback fight from his Achilles injury, on the other side of the world Lucas Browne was about to embark on his own career in the ring, at this point, though, in a mixed martial arts cage. He was about to do battle with a fellow big man,

Jim King, at Luna Park on the shores of Sydney's beautiful harbour. Not exactly an auspicious venue from which to launch a career. Uncertain about which way his fight career would take him, Browne mixed boxing bouts with his MMA fights to begin with. In 2009 he had five cage fights for five victories and, in between, made his professional boxing debut against Jason Kier at Manly Leagues Club for a fourth-round stoppage. In 2010 he had three MMA fights, including the losses to Cormier and York, and his second boxing bout, knocking Sam Leuii out in the first round. With trainer Tama Te Huna now guiding him, professional boxing was his chosen career path. All told, Browne had eight mixed martial arts fights for six victories and two technical knockout losses. Of those, seven bouts were fought concurrently with his first two boxing matches.

There was nothing too subtle about Browne's attitude or skill set. He didn't require too much else to get the job done than a big right hand. His first six boxing bouts went by in a blur, none lasting more than the four rounds it took him to knock out Kier.

His seventh fight took him to the Western Australian goldmining town of Kalgoorlie, where he fought his first ever twelve-round fight, being unable to land the killer knockout blow to Clarence Tillman. It was here that Browne was confronted by his own limitations. Tillman's defensive technique exposed Browne's over-reliance on his right hand to finish fights. Browne explains:

> Tillman was very effective with shoulder rolls in
> blocking my right hand, so much so that it almost

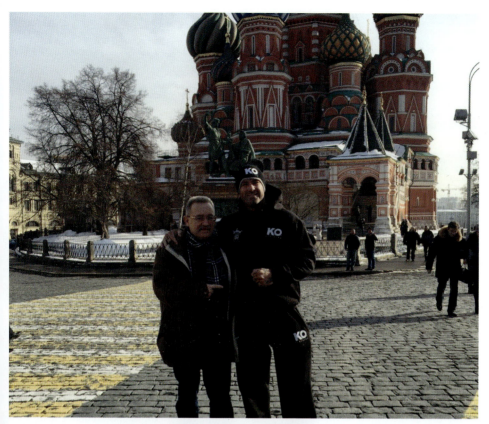

ABOVE: Lucas Browne and team member Philippe Fondu in Red Square, Moscow, prior to arriving in Grozny. The ornate St Basil's Cathedral is in the background.

LEFT: Lucas proudly displays the Australian flag that adorns the trunks he will don in the ring.

ABOVE: The view of modern Grozny from the 24th floor of Grozny City Hotel. In the foreground is the Islamic Centre and the magnificent Akhmad Kadyrov Mosque, the 'Heart of Chechnya'.

BELOW: The VADA testing on the Monday prior to the title fight. It came back negative to all banned substances.

ABOVE: Lucas Browne poses with a loaded handgun. Next to him is one of his smiling Chechen bodyguards, Abubakar.

LEFT: Adam Saidov sitting with a family friend, also named Adam. The elder Adam is clothed in Chechen national dress.

ABOVE: Father and son, Graham and Matt Clark, sharing lunch with Lucas Browne and trainer Rodney Williams in the restaurant atop Grozny City Hotel.

BELOW: The press conference two days out from the title fight. From left to right sit Pedro Diaz, Timur Dugazaev, Ruslan Chagaev, Alex Fedesov, Adam Saidov, Lucas Browne, Philippe Fondu and Matt Clark.

ABOVE: The world champion Ruslan Chagaev and his challenger Lucas Browne size each other up following the press conference. Russian event coordinator Alex Fedesov can be seen standing directly behind Chagaev.

LEFT: President Ramzan Kadyrov with Adam Saidov in the Akhmat Fight Club gym.

ABOVE: Philippe Fondu preparing Browne for the big fight. He is seen here wrapping the boxer's preferred weapon of choice, his heavy right hand.

BELOW: Chagaev's danger punch, his looping left hook, slips past Lucas Browne, giving the Australian the opportunity to respond with his powerful right: his knockout blow. (GETTY IMAGES)

ABOVE: Battered and bruised, but the new WBA heavyweight champion of the world, Lucas 'Big Daddy' Browne. He is flanked by Matt Clark (to his right) and Philippe Fondu (to his left). (GETTY IMAGES)

LEFT: A moment to savour. Adam Saidov stands with his new friend and now world champion, Lucas Browne. They pose beneath the billboard promoting the showdown.

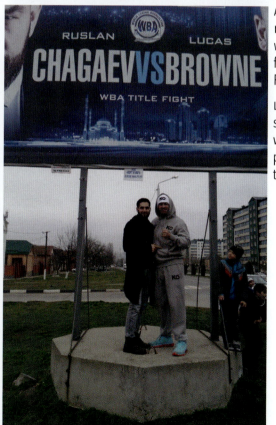

ABOVE: On the tarmac in Moscow with the legendary Kostya Tszyu. In the foreground with Kostya is Matt Clark. In the background, from left to right, stand Graham Clark, trainer Rodney Williams, the Browne brothers, Patrick, Danny and Lucas, and Matt Meyerhoff.

BELOW: The job's done. Lucas Browne permits himself to relax on the flight departing Russia. He will arrive home in Australia as the nation's very first world heavyweight boxing champion.

became null and void. I had to use my left to get
through and I didn't know what the hell I was doing.
I basically jabbed him for twelve rounds. I caught
about four punches the entire time, that's how much I
dominated it, but I couldn't knock him out because he
took my right hand out of the fight.

But the points victory did deliver Browne his very first
boxing belt, the UBC Inter-continental title. However, it was
to be his very next contest that Browne would regard as a
turning point in his burgeoning career.

He was pitted against a heavyweight from Auckland, Fai
Falamoe, at the Campbelltown Sports Club for the WBF
Asia Pacific title. Browne tells the story of that encounter
best himself:

It was the most worried I've ever been in a fight.
He was a big Islander from New Zealand, thick set
and an older-style fighter. I was smacking him with
some punches that dropped most other fighters and he
was just smiling at me. He'd then take a massive swing
at me and just miss my head. He just kept coming
and I started to wonder what I had to do to knock this
guy out.

By the fifth round, Browne was still moving around,
searching for the best angles, but he was tiring, so many big
bombs had he launched at Falamoe. Then, with the round
nearly over, he fired a huge right that caught his opponent
sweetly, sending him stumbling backwards against the referee

and then to the canvas. Browne's reaction was mostly relief: 'Yes, thank God that's over.'

But he felt he had passed some sort of test. He had been pushed out of his comfort zone, where what usually came easily to him just wasn't working. Still, in the end, it was the best tool in his kit bag, his stunning right hand, that won the day.

Lucas 'Big Daddy' Browne fought four times in 2012, over a total of eleven rounds. He scored three technical knockouts and one clean knockout of Colin 'Kid Coalminer' Wilson, securing him the Australian heavyweight title. He had reached a point in his career where he had complete confidence in his right hand against any opponent. This worked against him. His technique was not developing enough to provide him with a full arsenal of shots, if or when the right was not quite enough. And he knew himself that his fitness was never what it needed to be.

Yet here he was, the Australian heavyweight champion with a record of eleven professional fights for eleven wins, ten by knockout. The trend continued through his next four fights, scoring stoppage wins in all. Again, he did his work quickly and got out of there.

His next bout would pit him against the ageing American boxer James Toney at the Melbourne Convention Centre. At forty-four years of age, Toney was by no means the fighter he once was, but was still, without doubt, the classiest opponent that had yet to step into a ring with Browne. A world champion in three weight divisions, twice a contender for the world heavyweight championship, twice *Ring Magazine* fighter of the year, his pedigree was beyond question. In April

2005 he had lifted the WBA heavyweight title from John Ruiz, only to test positive to anabolic steroids post-fight. He was subsequently stripped of his title win, banned for ninety days and the belt was handed back to Ruiz. He came within a whisker of claiming the WBC title a year later, fighting a majority draw against Hasim Rahman. He had wins against Evander Holyfield and Fres Oquendo on his resume and he had what troubled Lucas Browne most: a tight defence.

As it turned out, the result was never in question. In what was expected to be a steep step-up in class for the Australian, Browne dominated throughout, winning every round on one judge's card. Although he was unable to land a knockout blow, Browne continually used his reach advantage on his shorter opponent, annoying him incessantly with his darting jab. Now his record read sixteen fights, sixteen wins, fourteen knockouts. He was getting noticed.

The examinations of what he was made of kept coming. Next he was to fight someone his own size and with similar power, Travis Walker, the American from Tallahassee, Florida, and was to find himself on the canvas in the first round, albeit just on his right knee from a glancing blow to the top of his head. Big Daddy responded by putting Walker down three times before ending the contest in the seventh.

With the former great world champion Ricky Hatton now promoting him, Browne's next target, in November 2013, was a showdown with Richard Towers in the Yorkshire city of Hull, the winner gaining a Commonwealth title shot. Nicknamed 'The Inferno', Towers stood over Browne, measuring 6 foot 8 inches or 203 centimetres. He fought out of the iconic St Thomas's gym in Wincobank, Sheffield, under the direction of local legend Brendan Ingle, so there was little doubt that he would be well schooled, with a hardened edge.

He and Browne were former sparring partners who had formed a friendship, so the Australian knew that Towers was aware of his power. Browne's camp was prepared for him to give away points in the early rounds as long as their fighter was working away at his opponent's body, setting him up for the knockout blow later on.

From the first round Browne went head-hunting, sensing that Towers wasn't keen on his power. He was throwing heavy punches in an attempt to finish his work quickly – and, by the break after the fourth round, Browne's corner reminded him fairly forcefully about his fight plan, to attack the body.

As he went out for the fifth, he threw a body shot and then went for the head. This time he stunned Towers with a heavy swinging left that bent him back over the top rope and now he had the Australian all over him, merciless and brutal. The referee stepped in, Towers stumbling and groggy.

Browne would fight again in a month's time, at Melbourne Pavilion. He met Clarence Tillman for a second time, on this occasion sweeping him aside in the second round.

A test of character came next: his bout with Eric Martel Bahoeli for the vacant Commonwealth heavyweight title. His fifth-round victory not only gave him the belt but also a record that was getting increasingly difficult to ignore: twenty fights, twenty wins, eighteen knockouts. When he faced the Ukrainian Andriy Rudenko in Wolverhampton, Browne was being spoken about as a world-title prospect. But before all those what ifs and maybes, he had an undefeated and confident Ukrainian standing in his way. For his part, Rudenko had little doubt about the likely outcome of this clash. 'I cannot say that he is something special. He is an ordinary slugger, so I expect a tough but predictable fight,' he said in advance of the fight.

And indeed, Browne looked down the barrel of defeat during this encounter for the very first time in his career and it was a sobering experience for him. He puts it this way:

> I came into the Rudenko fight at around 120 kilograms; ego played a big part in that. I was coming off the Bahoeli fight where I knocked him out and before that, Tillman only lasted into the second round after he took me to twelve in Kalgoorlie. I had those wins after coming off a high from my bout with Towers who was supposed to be the best thing since sliced bread. So my thinking was 'Okay, I've got the power, I'll knock him over easily.' As it turned out, it wasn't so easy.

They say that what doesn't kill you makes you stronger, and Browne arguably learned more from having to grind out a points victory than he would have from another dramatic early stoppage.

Now Lucas 'Big Daddy' Browne was ranked fifth-best heavyweight in the world by the World Boxing Association. The prospects of a world title tilt were starting to firm. Full of confidence, he swept aside Chauncy Welliver, the Kiwi-adopted American, when his faithful right hand closed his opponent's left eye, the ringside doctor ruling that he could not meet the bell for the sixth round.

In 2015 Browne was moved up to be the mandatory challenger to Chagaev's WBA regular title. He had arrived on the world scene. Negotiations commenced to bring the pair together, but, before that could come to pass, Chagaev had a commitment to meet Francesco Pianeta while Browne had an engagement with the towering American Julius Long.

Based in New Zealand, Long was known as the 'Towering Inferno', standing 7 feet 1 inch or an incredible 216 centimetres tall. Browne made hard work of this ten-round bout in Melbourne, finally securing the knockout in the penultimate round. His very first scoring punch had hit Long high on the forehead, his fist connecting at an awkward angle that broke his thumb. So from the start of the fight, Browne's best weapon was to a degree disabled.

Courage and force of will got him home and, suddenly, the path ahead to a world title fight lay open. Chagaev would be the opponent, having beaten Pianeta the month before.

Lucas 'Big Daddy' Browne would join Bill Squires, Bill Lang, Kali Meehan and Alex Leapai as the only Australians to ever contest a world heavyweight title. He had the chance to do what none of these boxers had done – win it.

VI. Shots at Glory

More than a century before Lucas Browne, two other Australian boxers had their eyes on a similar prize. Bill Squires and Bill Lang would both get their shots at glory against the reigning world champion, the Canadian Tommy Burns. Burns is best remembered for his loss to Jack Johnson in Sydney, but is credited in boxing history as the first truly international heavyweight champ. Burns took the defence of his world title across continents and was willing to step into the ring with any opponent, irrespective of race or creed.

Bill Squires was to get three shots at Tommy Burns' crown. The first came in July 1907 in California. Squires stepped into the ring as a red-hot favourite, the hype about his punching power preceding him. Back in Australia, he had put together a series of knockout victories, one of which delivered him the national title. Then three consecutive first-round stoppages secured him this coveted opportunity.

At 170 centimetres, the Canadian is the shortest heavyweight champion ever and many expected the Australian's strength to dominate him. But Burns had a punch to be respected, and in the very first round he sent the challenger to the canvas and the fight was over. Coming into the clash, Squires' record stood at twenty-three bouts for only one loss; following the knockout by Burns, his record read ten further bouts for nine losses. Many believed that Bill Squires was never quite the same fighter again following his disastrous defeat in his title bid.

Tommy Burns knocked Bill Squires out twice more, once in Paris in June 1908 and then again in Sydney two months later. Just two weeks later, the champion squared off against Bill Lang who would, nearly a century later, be inducted into the country's boxing hall of fame.

Lang's record wasn't as imposing as Squires', as he had suffered four losses from his twenty-two bouts prior to his showdown with the titleholder, but this time Burns knew he had been in a fight. The athletic Lang, just as devastating in his Richmond colours on an Australian Rules football field as he was in the ring, connected with a stunning left hook in the second round. However, Burns was made of stern stuff. He regained his feet and his composure to overwhelm Lang, knocking him out in the sixth round. The Canadian's next fight would be his last as the world champion, losing his title to Johnson on Boxing Day 1908.

As for Bill Lang, there was a lot more left in the tank following his failed title campaign; he had another twenty-one bouts for eleven wins. Four of those victories would be against his compatriot Bill Squires, all stoppages.

So there it was, the century newly born, just seven short years after the nation's federation and already two Australians had challenged for the most highly regarded prize in boxing, a heavyweight crown. Who would have thought then that it would be another ninety-six years before it would happen again?

Kali Meehan almost won a world title. At the end of his bruising encounter with the American Lamon Brewster for the WBO title in Las Vegas in September 2004, the judges' score cards read 115–113 Brewster, 114–113 Meehan, 114–113 Brewster. In a sport where the scoring is so subjective, many thought the challenger had done enough to take the fight and the world title. One of the three judges agreed. In the eighth round, Meehan had been all over the champion, catching him with a series of wicked right hands, but ultimately was unable to finish the job. The New Zealand–born challenger accepted the verdict with grace and moved on.

He had suffered only one defeat from his thirty bouts leading into the Brewster encounter and, coming out of it, he would record thirteen more victories, his only defeats to top-shelf fighters Hasim Rahman, Travis Walker, New

Zealand's promising heavyweight Joseph Parker and the selfsame Ruslan Chagaev.

Ten years after the Brewster–Meehan match-up, Logan City's Alex Leapai became the fourth Australian to earn his chance at writing his name in boxing's pages of history. Of proud Samoan heritage, Leapai scored a unanimous points win over contender Denis Boytsov in Germany to set up his challenge against the imposing master of the sport, the Ukrainian Wladimir Klitschko.

Of the four Australian boxers thus far, Leapai had arguably been assigned the toughest task, stepping into the ring with a fighter that many already considered a legend. Armed with an immaculate jab and a lethal right, Klitschko had a size and reach advantage over the challenger that most thought insurmountable.

The timing of the April 2014 event was inauspicious for Leapai. Just the month before, Russian forces annexed the Ukrainian territory of Crimea as part of the wider conflict between the two nations. An escalation in the war seemed more than possible. The world champion saw his contest against Leapai as his opportunity to lift the spirits of his countrymen and -women.

Klitschko proceeded to put on a clinical display of power jabbing and heavy right crosses and, together with his precise footwork and evasiveness, completely swamped the challenger. Leapai was knocked down three times before the referee stopped the contest in the fifth and, yet again, an Australian boxer had been denied the ultimate prize.

Alex Leapai would have only two more bouts following the Klitschko fight for two losses. His career was cut short by an early retirement in February 2016, with a specialist expressing concern for his eyesight.

When Lucas 'Big Daddy' Browne slid through the ropes in Grozny to face Ruslan Chagaev, he put his name alongside Bill Squires, Bill Lang, Kali Meehan and Alex Leapai as Australian challengers for a heavyweight title. If he were to win, his name would stand alone in the annals of Australian boxing.

CHAPTER SEVEN

A Seat at the Table

I. Grozny Chronicle – Friday, 4 March 2016

As we awake, a pea soup fog has descended. Light and noise struggle to penetrate the thick atmosphere of the early morning, with even the dawn call to prayer being slightly muffled. Today is the weigh-in and tonight the official ceremony and media 'weigh-in'. Lucas looks fresh and relaxed and, as one of the judges for the fight conceded to him yesterday, not someone you would want to step into a ring with.

The scene downstairs is ramping up as various languages echo through the breakfast room, everyone busy, going about their business in their small teams. There seems more purpose to everything that is happening, more urgency to conversations. We sit here now with less than forty hours before Lucas steps into the ring. You don't need to be too intuitive to sense the nervous energy that pervades the room, but Lucas, for his part, still exudes an inner calm that suggests he will not let the occasion overwhelm him.

Tomorrow is the day of days for Lucas. Today, routine steps aside for formality. Tonight there will be no opportunity for a gym workout as the official pre-fight ceremony will be held, hosted by President Kadyrov. And this morning, at 11 am, Lucas Browne and Ruslan Chagaev will weigh in for the bout. So after breakfast our entire team files into the small room on the second floor of our hotel, where the weigh-in is to take place.

When we arrive, boxers and their teams sit or traipse around the room, milling in small groups, talking, but with an apparent absence of purpose to proceedings. It seems to me that all of the fighters on the undercard have already weighed in and are now just passing time. The person absent from the room is Chagaev; his late arrival is what is holding up proceedings. It seems to be a pattern. In the meantime, Lucas sits at a small table where he undergoes the mandatory medical check before a fight, having his heart rate and blood pressure checked.

As we sit and wait, we meet Ali Funeka, the South African, who is a former IBO world welterweight champion. He is also a three-time challenger for the world lightweight title. For a fighter of his status, he seems refreshingly shy and humble. He will meet the unbeaten Russian welterweight Viskhan Murzabekov and promises to have a class and certainly an experience advantage over his rival. Now in walks an athlete of a different profile and personality.

Tyrone Spong fills a room with his outgoing nature and confident swagger. As approachable as Funeka, he is none too pleased with the stalled proceedings of the morning, but, unlike the Browne team, his commitments are now over. The Dutch-Surinamese veteran of eighty-three kickboxing fights and two MMA bouts, Spong is scheduled to have his third boxing match when he meets a fighter from neighbouring Georgia, David Gogishvili, on Saturday evening. He radiates a calm certitude of victory. The Chagaev team finally enters the room, the fighter hulking in, dressed in his black tracksuit, ahead of his genial trainer, Pedro Diaz, and the rest of his entourage, including Timur Dugazaev. With the champion in the room the event can proceed. He and Lucas are summoned to the scales. Onlookers gather round.

The weigh-in for a heavyweight bout is a strange thing, a ceremony without consequence, for there is no weight limit for heavyweights to meet. The battle is more psychological: how hard has each fighter trained, how much excess trim has he shed in the months of sacrifice leading up to this moment? The challenger steps onto the scales and tips them at 113.1 kilos – superb, the lightest and fittest he has fought at professionally. Lucas steps away, his face expressionless, not hinting at the inner satisfaction he feels. The champion moves onto the scales and he registers 112.5, up there with the heaviest he has fought at for some time. Another chess piece moved into place.

The fog has lifted, the sun shines brightly, but a storm is brewing.

With that formality done, some of us accompany Lucas back upstairs to our twenty-fourth floor. Matt, Rodney and Philippe stay at the venue to attend the WBA rules meeting, where the regulations for this world title fight will be clarified. The meeting will be led by WBA-appointed supervisor Renzo Bagnariol and also in attendance, apart from our team, are referee Stanley Christodoulou, Alex Fedesov, as well as Pedro Diaz and Timur Dugazaev from team Chagaev.

Matt soon reports back to us about the meeting. Subtle dramas continue to be played out this week with the finesse of a Shakespearean play. All world title fights walk hand-in-hand with melodrama, negotiation and push and shove, as teams angle for advantage or psychological scores before the fighters step into the ring. One thing I've been told over and over again by those who live their lives out in this sport is that boxing at this level is a cut-throat game, an environment where, if you're not sharp, alert and street smart, you can quickly be ground into the pavement. Smart fighters surround themselves with smart people.

As stipulated in the contractual arrangements for this fight, both boxers are to supply their own gloves and provide them for inspection by the rival team. When the gloves are tabled at the meeting, there is a noticeable size difference between the red gloves that Lucas will wear into the fight and the black pair that Chagaev will don. Both pairs are the same Mexican brand, Cleto Reyes, but Lucas's have been made specifically for him. They come with the Hatton Boxing logo emblazoned on them. They are smaller than Chagaev's.

Known in the sport as a puncher's glove, the leather casing of a Cleto Reyes is not cushioned with the standard foam padding, but instead is filled with horsehair. A fighter whose best tool is a knockout punch would choose this brand of glove believing that the horse hair imparts the undiluted, raw power of his fists most effectively.

The champion's trainer, Pedro Diaz, immediately questions the legitimacy of the gloves, asserting that they do not appear to be the correct weight. Philippe confidently counters that the gloves are the standard 10 ounces. When he is proven correct, the gloves are initialled and sealed in bags, where they will stay, under guard by the WBA, until they are delivered to our change room tomorrow night.

The rest of the meeting is uneventful, but essential. The rules for the WBA fight will be standard: the three-knockdown rule is in effect, meaning that three knockdowns in one round by one boxer wins him the bout. Only the referee can stop the fight; an injured boxer cannot lose from an intentional foul; there will be a five-minute recovery time from a low blow; only three team members are allowed on the ring apron; and surgical tape must be one inch behind the fist knuckle. Like a freight train rolling downhill, the fight looms ever closer.

Lucas kicks back for an afternoon snooze while we head once again to the markets. We shuffle through the vibrant, bustling alleyways, the vendors polite and helpful, never harassing. Spicy aromas, tempting merchandise, Chechen chitchat, the pride and honesty of the vendors, fellow shoppers flocking to Rodney who is trying to pass himself off as Usher or Floyd Mayweather – it is a pleasure to experience.

No gym work tonight; Lucas is primed and ready to explode. It's deep in tapering time. There is nothing to do physically; the battle now is mental. Lucas seems to be meeting that challenge as well: he's cool, laid-back and in control.

Our van takes us to the official ceremony and media weigh-in. Heavily armed security swarm everywhere; the Chechens mean business tonight. An armed guard boards our van and scans our faces as we sit in nervous silence.

Finally he is satisfied and signals our entrance to the grounds of the hall.

The venue, Safia Palace, matches the occasion, spectacularly ornate in the style of a Parisian opera house. We parade through the foyer, which is adorned with huge images of each fighter on the card. Soon we are plunged into a cultural feast that amazes, excites and bewilders, while President Kadyrov sits just metres away from us, the American announcer Michael Buffer by his side. The president's three young sons sit at the table between ours and their father's.

The event is as lavish as the venue. Waiters hover over each table, at our beck and call. We eat finger foods from platters while Lucas, along with every fighter, has a specially prepared meal served to him. A waiter arrives at our table to serve only two people, the pair of combatants, Lucas and Brian Minto. Before Lucas is placed a steak, a meal fit for a future world champion. In a memorable moment one of the African fighters is heard to excitedly exclaim, wide smile on his face, 'I am eating cow!'

It is an unsettling comment: our privileged lives, which we accept without question, are exposed by his guileless enthusiasm and delight.

The meal over, the formalities commence. Each boxer is to be announced from the stage, upon which they are to stride to the podium and, in a mock process, stand on the scales that are not actually measuring anything at all, and pose as boxers sometimes do: chest out, biceps flexed. But the weigh-in carries an important difference from the ones we are used to seeing: the boxers are fully clothed. This, remember, is a Muslim place.

As each boxer takes to the scales, the image of his face on the big screen behind gives way to an image of whirling numbers. Finally the screen settles, the image clarifies and the fighter's weight is there for all to see. The Chechen compere then announces the weight dramatically – the weight that was actually registered at the Grozny City Hotel this morning. The audience applauds and the boxer returns to his seat.

That is, if the fighter is not Chechen or an Uzbek bearing the name Ruslan Chagaev. If either is the case, his journey to the stage is much more dramatic. When he is summoned, he will arrive by chauffeured car outside the venue and the audience will track his journey to join us on the video screen.

I am sitting next to Adam when the process begins and the first African boxer is announced. He stands and moves to the stage and approaches the mock scales. No one has informed him what is actually happening here and, as he loiters next to the scales, he begins to disrobe, his shirt coming off and his tracksuit bottoms are discarded, as boxers do when trying to meet a weight limit. There are audible groans from Chechen authorities near us. Adam sits bolt upright and whispers more to himself than to anyone else, 'Oh no. No. This is … oh no!'

In distress Adam races the twenty or thirty metres to the stage and, taking off his suit jacket, shields the fighter's body from the audience as he puts his clothes back on. The African was not to know; obviously someone neglected to inform his team as to what was happening here. I imagine the fact that this occurred in front of President Kadyrov has made it all the more embarrassing for all concerned.

We arrive at the main event. Lucas is announced to warm applause and the big man stands at our table and strides to the stage. Video footage runs on the screen above, showing the punching machine at work, the footage recorded at the Akhmat gym on Tuesday evening. When the master of ceremonies concludes his introduction of Lucas, he steps onto the 'scales'. The image spins, the melodrama builds and the weight appears, 113.75 kilograms. Inexplicably, Lucas has gained 650 grams in the cyber world since this morning.

Now Ruslan Chagaev, in his home territory, is heralded by Chechen music and extraordinary Cossack-style dance while the video shows him arriving outside the venue by vintage car. We all wait as the champion winds his way through the foyer, up the stairs, into the hall and up onto the stage. He goes through the process and his weight is the correct 112.5 kilograms. With champion and challenger standing side by side on stage, the Australian turns to the Uzbek and offers his hand. Chagaev hesitates and then responds. Mind games or just an innocent incident of a fighter not knowing what to make of an unexpected gesture of sportsmanship? Who knows, but maybe Lucas won the moment anyway, being himself while possibly taking his opponent slightly out of his comfort zone. Lucas makes his way back to our table and Chagaev to his exalted position at the president's table.

The tempo of the music builds, its rhythm irresistible, and soon we are all standing, clapping and swaying to its beat, in an enclosed circle around the dancers.

Without warning, Special Forces–style military men stealthily glide around the room, balaclavas masking their faces, automatic weapons in hand, eyes fixed on their leader. They encircle the crowd, alert, a dark, ominous sense of pernicious intent about their movement as they glide like serpents, predators on the prowl. As alien and menacing as the sight behind me is, the spectacle before me is even more hypnotic, and my eyes are drawn back to the graceful dancers who seem to glide upon the floor rather than step.

Then, either in a prearranged or improvised moment, the dancers give up their floor to their master. The dancers become the audience with us, enlarging the circle, now spectators to their president. Ramzan Kadyrov is the complete centre of attention once again. Now he is the one dancing, strutting and gesturing, rhythmical and balanced, at the centre of the circle. Around and around the circle he swirls with one of the chosen female dancers, sublimely happy in the attention showered upon him.

His attention diverts to the small group of Australians in the circle and he dances towards Lucas. Stepping ever closer, eyes set on the challenger, he glides towards him as if to bring the focus of attention with him to share with Lucas. Or is it to intimidate the challenger? Just last night, the president did hit the Australian without warning, but tonight, he smiles and moves away, a joke shared between two combatants.

Ruslan Chagaev sits in his position at President Kadyrov's table, a place he has earned by being the craftsman of the ring that he has been for more than fifteen years. Tomorrow night, Lucas 'Big Daddy' Browne will get his chance. Being the Aussies we are, we are the last to leave. Back in the foyer *of our hotel, a Russian associate of Michael Buffer is jumping on board the Browne bandwagon, offering to 'look after' him in Moscow. Lucas hasn't much time for spotlight-seekers or backslappers, be they big-time players or nobodies.*

Back on the twenty-fourth floor, Lucas and Pat sit together on the bed and talk, drifting towards stories of their childhood, the boys' adventures that have bonded them. Pat, the youngest of the three Browne boys, is quieter than his brothers, happy to step back and concede the stage to them, but he is equally sincere, intelligent and talented. A songwriter, Pat speaks from the heart. Danny, ever keen on more adventure, leaves with Matt, Rod and Adam to seek a karaoke bar and taste more of the new Grozny. We all feel extremely fortunate to have experienced this reborn city, with its intoxicating mix of culture, history and Western-style development. I feel grateful to Browne who has, through his ability and charismatic nature, invited me into our very own When We Were Kings odyssey.

It is about one in the morning as I record all the events of this memorable day. As I recall the champion sitting at President Kadyrov's table this evening, I am left with the thought of the opportunity that has opened up for Lucas. A victory will win him a seat at a far more sought-after table than the one Chagaev sat at tonight. It is a seat at the table of Australian world champions. He would have to climb to the top of the mountain to sit there. So I consider his perilous final ascent of that mountain face, the dangers that lurk, both on his climb and in his own mind, and finally I reflect on the story of one man, someone who has worked behind the scenes to make Lucas Browne's climb a reality.

II. Chase Just One Rabbit

The roll call of great American boxers of the later 1950s and early '60s – Sugar Ray Robinson, Jake LaMotta, Rocky Marciano, Floyd Patterson and Sonny Liston – is etched deep in the memory of boxing fans all over the world. But in the memory of Philippe Fondu, whose lifelong fascination with the art of the ring began in those years, the names that live in his memory are altogether different – names such as Jean Sneyers, Cyrille Delannoit, Louis Van Hoeck and Kid Dussart.

Fondu sat in venues such as the Palais des Sports and Saint Sauveur in Brussels with his grandfather, watching, riding the big hits, dodging the big blows, as Belgian boxing enjoyed its glory days. Like many others who fall in love with the sport, he eventually had to try his own hand in the amateur ranks, training and fighting in Brussels while studying dentistry at university. There was to be no career in the ring for him. However, once the bug had bitten, there was no escape.

Through his involvement in the community service organisation Kiwanis Club, Fondu – whose role in Browne's corner on Saturday night could make or break his title bid – became involved in promoting boxing dinners, with the proceeds assisting charities and worthwhile causes. At the same time, he opened a small boxing club in the garage of his home in Saint-Josse-ten-Noode, in central Brussels, and developed a few handy amateur fighters, some who won national championships. Working his dental practice in the day and running his boxing club at night, Fondu's life was full, but he somehow also found the time to promote three or four boxing events a year.

As some of his young boxers turned professional, they asked Fondu to manage them – and a door was opening onto his future in the game. In his new role, he began to develop international contacts, working in close relationships with some of the most well-known promoters and managers of the time – Jean Bretonnel of France, Henk Ruhling from Holland, Mickey Duff from the UK and South Africans Rodney Berman and Cedric Kushner. From them he learned the trade of securing opportunities for his boxers in venues throughout Europe and in South African cities such as Durban, Sun City and Johannesburg.

Despite the restrictions of apartheid, South Africa was enjoying a thriving professional boxing scene in the 1980s and Fondu took many of his fighters there. In Fondu's opinion, one of the pivotal reasons for the South African boom at that point was the ability and character of the man in charge. The head of the South African Boxing Board then was Stanley Christodoulou who, more than twenty-five years later, would be in Grozny with Fondu as the third man in the ring with Chagaev and Browne.

Fondu recalls Christodoulou's standards and sense of discipline:

I remember like it was yesterday an official weigh-in
that was scheduled for twelve o'clock in Johannesburg.
A heavyweight who had been travelling by car from a
far-flung location arrived fifteen minutes late for his
commitment. Stanley told the kid 'the fight's off, next
time you'll be on time'.

Another door opened for Fondu in the autumn of 1990 when he chased a different passion of his, hunting wild boar in the forests of Bulgaria. It was shortly after the fall of the communist regime led by Todor Zhivkov, and, suddenly, Bulgarian amateur fighters had the option of turning pro and trying to make a living from their craft. For Fondu it was a matter of being in the right place at the right time and he found himself at the centre of developing pro boxing in Bulgaria, Ukraine and Russia.

Learning Bulgarian and Russian allowed him to sign several promising boxers from the former Eastern Bloc, fighters such as Martin Krastev, the first Bulgarian professional to become a European champion, and, later, Tontcho Tontchev, who had given the future immortal Oscar De La Hoya such a hard fight in the quarterfinals of the Barcelona Olympics in 1992. Fondu's connections continued to widen, joining forces with French promoters Michel and Louis Acaries, travelling and negotiating in exotic destinations like Monaco, Cayenne, Martinique and Guadeloupe. By this stage Fondu had committed himself fully to his boxing responsibilities, closing his dental practice. Boxing was now not just his passion, it was his career.

The Belgian readily identifies one of his greatest strengths a factor that has made him so successful in his trade.

'I have always been willing to go where boxing has taken me,' he says.

When interest in boxing in France waned, he packed his bags and headed to the United Kingdom and joined the team of Frank Maloney and Panos Eliades of Panix Promotions, their stable including many promising up-and-comers, among them Lennox Lewis. He worked on promotions in Britain and in places as far afield and different as Uganda and Las Vegas, Namibia and Los Angeles.

But it was in Eastern Europe that Fondu cemented his reputation as a big player in the behind-the-scenes negotiations so fundamental to boxing. He later teamed up with the president of the National Boxing League of Ukraine, Mikhail Zavialov, managing a talented stable of boxers, promoting events throughout the world. By then, he was a skilled communicator, multilingual and fully conversant in the art of achieving outcomes for his boxers.

As he puts it: 'The ranking process is a relationship process.' The connections he established, the trust that he built and the knowledge of people that he garnered over the years transformed this Belgian dentist into a boxing kingmaker. One thing that he understood clearly is that unless you have an outright superstar on your hands, you have to bargain and argue your fighter's way up the rankings.

Lesser mortals require more than compiling victories in the ring to secure a big opportunity. A smart management team ensures that the wins in the ring have some credibility about them and that the boxer's status is acknowledged by a boxing body's ranking. It is here, behind closed doors, in quiet discussions in an office or in the hectic business of conventions or executive meetings, that Fondu excels.

He is persistent, he knows his business, he is a superb communicator and he reads people well; any boxer that he represents has an excellent chance of rising through the rankings, as long as the victories keep coming.

Lucas 'Big Daddy' Browne's ranking by the WBA rose steadily, until in 2015 he became the official challenger to Ruslan Chagaev's world crown. Fondu focused on the WBA's ranking of Browne, his team recognising that opportunities lay ahead down that pathway. Browne's ranking did not enjoy the same meteoric rise within other bodies – just the WBA. As Fondu puts it, 'You've got to make sure you are chasing just one rabbit and not four rabbits at a time' – referring to the three other major boxing organisations, the WBO, the WBC and the IBF.

As far back as 2011, Browne's manager, Matt Clark, had made contact with Fondu in relation to a boxer that the Belgian then managed. Clark had established a network of contacts in the fight game and was enjoying some success in matchmaking, on this occasion seeking an opponent for Anthony Mundine.

Though nothing came of this first contact, Fondu was looking for a suitable opponent for middleweight Martin Murray. Clark managed to secure the Australian Peter Mitrevski Jr, who gave the future world title challenger a gruelling twelve-round contest.

From there, Clark and Fondu struck up a good working relationship. Fondu was matching plenty of bouts for Hatton Promotions and when Lucas Browne defeated Colin Wilson to win his Australian title, Clark enquired about whether Hatton Promotions were interested in taking Browne on board. Fondu responded that they were – and a way forward had just been cleared for the Australian heavyweight.

So in 2015, with Browne knocking out his opponents in WBA-sanctioned bouts, Fondu was given the leverage he needed to help deliver the Australian a shot at a world heavyweight title in Grozny. And Fondu would be there in the Chechen capital, in Lucas Browne's corner, as the vastly experienced cuts man that he had become.

Boxing has been in his blood for more than fifty years. It is his passion and his life's work, whether wheeling and dealing on the big stage or in the frantic frontlines stuff of being a cornerman. As Fondu sees it, the addiction of boxing has no cure.

'Once someone is bitten by the bug of this game, he will never be healed.'

Many years before, while on holiday in Miami, Florida, Fondu rang the number of a boxing immortal, optimistically dreaming that he would receive a positive response. Angelo Dundee, the trainer and cornerman for some of the giants of the sport, such as Muhammad Ali, Sugar Ray Leonard and George Foreman, answered. What's more, he immediately invited Fondu to his office. They chatted for hours, Fondu's aspirations growing and horizons widening as he listened to the famous trainer.

In the days that followed, Fondu's holiday became an elite master's degree in cornerman craft, delivered by the best in the business at his Fifth Street gym. Dundee showed him how to wrap a boxer's hands effectively and taught him the subtleties of attending to cuts and bruises. He introduced Fondu to an Enswell, the metal eye iron that is chilled and applied to a fighter's injury to decrease blood flow to the site. Fondu would look back at this time spent with Dundee as pivotal in his life, helping transform him into the highly skilled operator that he is today. Fondu's career has seen him rub shoulders with giants and walk the lonely journey with the foot soldiers of this uncompromising sport, both in equal measure. He has experienced the euphoria that it promises and the tragedy that it sometimes delivers. He is above all else a realist; he knows better than most that the game spins on the power of the dollar. Boxers in the end can be just a commodity, their worth assessed by their drawing power, their value retained for as long as their talent shines.

But from time to time, boxing rises above that and becomes something better. It is when the power of the human spirit proves irresistible, when it refuses to wilt before the obstacles placed in front of it and, in its triumph, inspires others to believe. That's what Philippe Fondu was looking for in Grozny.

III. Never Fear Fear

'Never fear fear. It can be your best friend in the boxing ring.'

Trainer Johnny Lewis, the elder statesman of Australian boxing, knows just about everything that there is to know about the make-up of a fighter and a champion. Once inside the ring, facing your opponent, there are only the skills that you possess and what lies within. He knows about mental toughness, he knows about defeating the opponent from within before defeating the one in the ring and he knows about 'climbing the mountain'. The 'fear' that he talks about here is to do with respect: recognising and dealing with your opponent's strengths. It can make the fighter sharper, prepared and ready. Johnny Lewis admired the journey that Lucas Browne had taken. On that Friday night before the big bout, Lucas Browne betrayed no outward signs of fear. If, however, fear *had* secreted itself away somewhere deep within him, it would have been fear of a particular type; not fear of his opponent or the battle that loomed, and not fear of the occasion and the possibility of freezing in the headlights.

His fear would be to do with himself. Browne's fear would be detected in nagging self-doubts about his work and effort of the past few months. Had he done enough? Was he fit enough? Despite his superb physical condition, it was a recurring theme for Browne:

> I don't think I push myself to the absolute limit, not
> yet anyway. During my whole career, I don't think I've
> ever been as fit as I need to be, including this world
> title fight.

If Lewis had been in conversation with Browne that night he probably would have complimented him on his condition, rather than questioned it. He would have seen the result of his months of bull-headed determination, a leaner, even stronger-looking Lucas Browne. And maybe he would have shared some of his insight and wisdom, garnered over the years of mentoring the unparalleled careers of the like of Jeff Fenech and Kostya Tszyu. According to the great trainer, a victory in the Chechen ring the next night would mark the *beginning* of his challenge, not an end. 'You start climbing once you have reached the top of the mountain. You climb just to make sure you stay there and don't start climbing down.'

In the days leading up to the fight, Lucas Browne received support from around the world of heavyweight boxing.

Former champion Hasim Rahman, the conqueror of Lennox Lewis, was so confident that Browne would prevail in the ring in Grozny that he congratulated him prematurely:

> I believe Lucas will win the WBA title in his next
> fight, so let me congratulate him in advance. This is a
> monumental accomplishment and I'm proud of Lucas.
> Welcome to the fraternity, my brother.

Rahman believed that Browne's size and power would get him home. So did Lucas Browne's namesake, Riddick Bowe, who shared the moniker 'Big Daddy'. 'Lucas is going to rock Ruslan Chagaev with that big right hammer of his and get hold of the WBA belt that I once proudly owned.'

And then to top it off, arguably the biggest name in modern heavyweight boxing, Tyson Fury, threw his support behind the challenger:

> He's fresher, let's say that. He's unbeaten and he's a
> knockout artist. Hopefully big Lucas wins. I know
> Chagaev obviously. I've watched him box for a long
> time, but he's been there and done that. He's too old. I
> want to see a new face with a new title.'

A man who would provide expert analysis on the British pay-per-view channel BoxNation was Steve Lillis. He had seen Browne fight, and only had praise for the big man:

> The courage of Lucas Browne has never been in
> question. We have seen him dig deep in Britain before

when he was badly cut against Eric Bahoeli. When he faced Andriy Rudenko on BoxNation, it looked like he might lose, but he dug deep in the late stages to snatch a deserved points win. Fans here totally respect him. They will always love a trier who puts it on the line, whether he is a four-rounder or in a world title fight. In his British fights, fans warmed to his fan-friendly style and for those who met him, either fans or people like me who work in the trade – I have never heard a bad word said about him as a person.

Perhaps the most perceptive forecast came from Australia's own Ben Damon, the well-known Main Event announcer and sports journalist who saw the big man's prospects this way:

> Browne is arguably the hardest puncher in world boxing, and under new trainer Rodney Williams he has developed his footwork to the extent of being a genuine chance against the slick and powerful Chagaev. This is an once-in-a-lifetime event as an Aussie tries to bring home a version of the biggest title of them all. And he goes into the fight with a punch that can make history. My tip: Browne's thunderous right hand to shock the boxing world and breathe gloriously brutal new life into Australian boxing.

For all of the support and confidence of others, the fact remained that, if Lucas 'Big Daddy' Browne were to triumph, it was to be there in Chechnya, in a place that had taken him way out of his comfort zone. Ruslan Chagaev sat at the president's table, on the champion's throne, a battle-hardened warrior at ease in the security of his own territory. If the challenger were to lift his crown, he would have to do it on the champion's turf.

IV. Fighting a Fighting Nation

When a boxer steps into the ring, he has just one man to beat – but he might find that he is fighting an entire nation. That's how it was for Browne, for his opponent was inextricably bound to Chechnya's president, who was likewise deeply enmeshed with the people of his country.

Both Ramzan Kadyrov and his father, Akhmad, fought with their countrymen against the Russians in the First Chechen War. The Kadyrovs, like many Chechens in military uniform, switched allegiances during the second conflict, in 1999. The second war was fought by separatists, Islamists and militants, splitting the country. Kadyrov senior, a mufti and religious scholar, was at odds with the Wahhabi strain of Islam, hence his switch to the Russians. Installed as the administrative head of Chechnya in 2000 by Vladimir Putin – who now ruled Russia as its president – he was elected Chechen president in 2003. His reign was short-lived, due to a terrorist bomb the following year.

Ramzan immediately became deputy prime minister and in 2007 was appointed president by Putin, which the Chechen parliament ratified. He was just thirty years of age, the minimum permitted under the Chechen Republic's constitution. Fighting men, leading a fighting people.

President Kadyrov no doubt enjoys Vladimir Putin's support through his demonstrated ability to maintain control and stability over the state. To this point, his military strength has proven more than capable of dealing with any threats posed by rebel groups or fundamental extremists.

As a military leader, Ramzan's men were the Kadyrovsty – 'Kadyrov's guys'. Essentially they are his own private militia, comprised of highly trained ex-army officers, police and war veterans. He once said of the Kadyrovsty: 'Look at them. American uniforms, Russian weapons, Islamic beliefs and a Chechen spirit. They are invincible.'

Russian roubles have poured into Chechnya, rebuilding and re-energising the country's economy, allowing President Kadyrov to cement his grip on power. As well as further beefing up his military forces, he has overseen major redevelopment. Towering buildings have been constructed, broad avenues and modern highways have been laid, a Western-style consumer culture of shopping and cafes has been cultivated and the fine arts have been patronised.

But unemployment remains high, the media is tightly controlled and freedom of expression is discouraged. Websites are scrutinised and blocked by the Interior Ministry, television and radio stations are state-controlled, while the local news outlet, Grozny Inform, is also a government agency. The Kadyrov name is synonymous with power, control and strong leadership.

One of the popular projects that the president has initiated is the building of the Akhmat Fight Club, the hub of boxing and mixed martial arts in Chechnya.

A fighting spirit is part of the make-up of the Chechen people, so it comes as no surprise that the president patronises boxing as he does. There are few presidents or political leaders who could handle the boxing gloves as he can and even fewer who would 'discipline' one of his ministers by stepping into a boxing ring with him. Kadyrov explained the sparring session with Salambek Ismailov, his sport and physical culture minister, with a post on social media: 'With a left and a right hook, I explained to him that you need to use your head.'

So if any fighter was to challenge the president's adopted boxing hero, Ruslan Chagaev, it was always going to be personal. Chagaev would enter the Colosseum Sports Hall ring with the complete moral and physical support of the president. In a country where security rests on a knife edge, it could be an intimidating factor working against a challenger.

Yet despite the loaded situation that Browne had accepted, despite the constant presence of heavy weapons, militia and security staff, Browne's experience in Grozny had been overwhelmingly inviting, characterised by warmheartedness. Vendors, people in the streets and fight fans in general had been nothing less than gracious, some even siding with the challenger. His experience of Muslim culture in Grozny reassured him, rather than discomforted him. He was welcomed into mosques with a humble gentleness that moved him.

The only violence he had experienced at all was just a punch from a president. As unconventional as that incident was, perhaps in President Kadyrov's mind, and according to Chechen standards, it was merely a playful act in front of the television cameras, almost a mark of respect from one veteran to another – with perhaps an undertone of the 'top dog' marking out his territory.

V. Overcoming the Odds

There is of course nothing unusual about a boxing match that involves a spiteful atmosphere. Some of Browne's supporters and admirers could tell a few stories about adverse conditions.

Johnny Lewis would nominate Kostya Tszyu's fight against the six-time world champion Julio Cesar Chavez in Phoenix, Arizona, in 2000. Well past his best, Chavez went to Phoenix followed by a crowd of fanatical supporters, all wishing to see their fading champion triumph. That Tszyu swamped the Mexican and scored a sixth-round TKO was cause for near chaos in the venue.

Lewis tells it this way:

Julio Cesar Chavez put a smile on a lot of Mexican faces, people who had done it tough over the years. He was just so popular. But he shouldn't have been in there with Kostya. I thought it had long ago gone past him. There were a lot of broken hearts that night when he finally succumbed to Kostya's punching power. They were pissing in cups and throwing them over at us. One of our seconds got king hit on the way back to the room and they kept us there a good hour until the crowd finally dispersed. But I think we were on a high and you don't smell fear too much when you win.

BoxNation's Steve Lillis was at Madison Square Garden when Britain's Michael Jennings challenged the great Puerto Rican champion Miguel Cotto for the WBO welterweight crown. It was quite a night. Jennings somehow managed to incite two nationalities that evening, both turning against him. Of course the Puerto Ricans would have been in Cotto's corner to begin with. Lillis explains:

> The Puerto Ricans were booing because he was taking on their hero. There were also thousands of Irish-Americans there to support John Duddy [in another fight]. Many were hateful. The crowd were still jeering when Jennings had taken his beating. Coming out to 'Anarchy in the UK' really riled the crowd up.

Australian boxing analyst Ben Damon could tell the big man a story about another courageous Australian fighter who travelled overseas, basically friendless, facing not only an intimidating environment but a big-name opponent. In September 2012, Australia's Daniel Geale travelled to Oberhausen in Germany to face the local hero, the formidable Felix Sturm. Geale was the reigning IBF middleweight champion of the world and Sturm held the WBA belt. Sturm would eventually go on to be Germany's only four-time world champion and, when he faced the Australian, he already had three titles to his name.

Damon was in Geale's corner that night and describes the setting for the bout like this:

Daniel was given very little chance in that fight. He doesn't travel with a big entourage or get involved in the hype that often surrounds world championship boxing. In the venue and in the change room that evening, it was a very claustrophobic atmosphere because there were a lot of very passionate Germans who most certainly did not want Daniel Geale to feel in any way welcome or comfortable.

The pressure did not end there, but extended to little mind games played out ringside. Damon continues:

Even when we got inside the ring prior to the fight there was an obvious move towards intimidation from those in the Sturm camp. There were some tricks being played behind the scenes, with the disappearance of bottles of water and the wrong gloves arriving. These are all elements that can easily play a role in intimidating or putting off a boxer overseas. Sometimes that slight apprehension can be decisive.

Geale soaked it all up, refused to be bullied and got on with the job. He scored a memorable victory, unifying the IBF and WBA world middleweight titles. Damon says:

Overcoming the odds is never easy, but I'll be forever impressed with how together Daniel Geale kept it that night. His boxing performance was remarkable and he completely overcame all those elements to produce a totally famous victory for an Australian.

Lucas Browne would have to do the same to triumph in Grozny; he would have to shut out all those distractions. He would have to keep it all together and stay focused. He would have to fight his fight in the ring and not in his mind.

From the outset, Browne had insisted that going to Grozny did not faze him:

> To me it's just a place I have to go to if I want to fulfil
> my dream of being a world champion. The crowd will
> be against me and I'm fine with that. I've been in hostile
> situations in my personal life so this holds no fear for me.

And there was one other factor at play here. Whether the bout was in Grozny or some darkened backstreet in Sydney's nightclub precinct, he knew one sure way to beat the odds: knock out his opponent. He believed that the lethalness of his feared right hand didn't diminish simply because the ring happened to be in Grozny, with a rabid crowd baying for his downfall.

'I've got the power to knock over anyone on the planet.'

CHAPTER EIGHT

And the Bell Rings

I. Grozny Chronicle – Saturday, 5 March 2016

The day has arrived. The sun has risen over Grozny and instinctively we all gravitate to Lucas's room before breakfast. As we look from the window of his room, the Colosseum Sports Hall can be clearly seen amid the cityscape, standing regally, snuggled in beside the football stadium, the Akhmat Arena. The arena is the home venue for the local football club FC Terek, which competes in the Russian Premier League, in which Australian Luke Wilkshire plays. Akhmat Arena has seating for 30,000 spectators and was the venue for Ruslan Chagaev's successful defence of his title against Fres Oquendo. It was also the scene of Akhmad Kadyrov's assassination twelve years ago.

But it is the Colosseum that catches our eye this morning. Its architecture demands attention: sleek, circular and imposing. From our distant vantage point, it has the aura of a place where important things happen.

Tonight, Lucas Browne will do battle there for the WBA regular heavyweight title of the world.

Over breakfast small talk dominates, but inevitably our conversation weaves its way to the big event, now only fifteen-odd hours away. Lucas himself knows that he can fight this bout in many ways. Move early, stay out of the way of heavy shots in the initial rounds, snap out his jab. Later launch the big shots, those rib- or liver-crunching left rips or the 'lights out' right crosses or those wicked right uppercuts or maybe, just maybe, keep moving, jabbing, accumulating points, clawing in the ascendancy and, after twelve gruelling rounds, a victory on points.

Rodney makes note of the importance of assessing Chagaev in the ring before the fight. If he is sweating, he's warmed up, fit and ready to go. But if he isn't, maybe he's not as fit as he could be and intends to use the early rounds to work his way into it. If so, there could be an opening for Lucas to go at him early, take advantage of any slight stiffness, fire the big ones at him and take him out then and there.

So here we find ourselves on the day of destiny for this big man, this boy from Sydney's west, this man who has journeyed to this city of contradiction, deep in the Caucasus, with the chance to do what no other Australian fighter has managed to do in boxing history. The only thing that we are all certain of is that Lucas 'Big Daddy' Browne will leave nothing unspent inside that ring tonight.

Lucas limbers up in the hallway with light drills, just to keep the feet moving, the body relaxed and the mind occupied. He steps out on the floor ladder and skips around the upright cups, alone in the hallway with his innermost thoughts, save for me, sitting, watching, taking it all in.

He may be a little more introspective than usual, but is not weighed down by nerves. I wonder what Chagaev is doing now. Does a veteran world champion have his set rhythm of preparation, drills and routines that has delivered him success so many times before? If so, has he followed them for this showdown, is his lead-up as precisely tuned as he would wish? And how seriously has the champion considered his Australian opponent? Has living in presidential luxury been an appropriate lead-up to this contest? While Lucas has been seen and embraced on the backstreets of Grozny, the world champion has been tucked away in a palace, far removed from the public eye. Whether he has been wrapped in cotton wool or pushing himself to the limits, one can only guess.

Meanwhile Rodney, Matt and Philippe plan the corner for tonight's fight. They will be the three-man team on the apron: Rodney, responsible for strategy, talking and guiding Lucas through the fight; Philippe on cuts and swellings; Matt doing the unnoticed but vital tasks, sliding the stool in and out of the blue corner, withdrawing the fighter's protective guard and mouthguard and cooling his head and neck with iced towels and sponges. Removing a boxer's protective guard allows his diaphragm to expand, letting him take deeper breaths to supply re-energising oxygen to his lungs. The ice treatment is essential for a boxer who has suffered before from elevated core body temperature during his fights.

And there's a possibility that Philippe could be busy in his job when you consider Lucas's past record of cuts. Philippe's associate, the Frenchman Alexandre Komurian, will be ringside monitoring the timing of the rounds and I will stand beside Matt Meyerhoff and Lucas's brothers, Danny and Pat, ensuring that Matt has those towels and sponges in his hands when he needs them. Rodney tells me later to take them out of the bucket when I hear the ten-second warning bell and wring them out; we don't want dripping water making the corner a slippery hazard. And no sooner than ten seconds – they need to be as icy cold as possible to serve their purpose.

We all sit for lunch at 2 pm, less than ten hours until the big occasion, and the mood is business as usual. Again, the afternoon sun warms the greenhouse in which we sit, making for a dull, lazy feeling of wellbeing. All of Lucas's work has been done, those long months of sweating in the BKH and Blacktown PCYC gyms, the plotting of a campaign, the believing when believing was perceived by others as blind optimism, the remodelling of a technique and the countless rounds of sparring, hitting and being hit. All finished, all in the bank, nothing left undone. So as we sit reclined in the filtered sunlight on comfortable lounge chairs, waiting for our lunch to be served, we sit in the company of a boxer who we know will give this world title one hell of a shake. We eat our final meal in the plush opulence of the thirty-second floor restaurant. We plan to leave for the venue at 6.30 pm, Lucas having no need for a heavy meal hours before he steps into the ring. The young waiter, as is his pleasant habit, plods hesitantly through the process of taking our orders, but nods his understanding with a confidence betrayed by his previous mistakes. Over lunch Danny is the master in keeping anxieties at bay and laughter flowing. He is the release valve for his brother, treating the occasion with sibling irreverence at times, but with his pride in his younger brother always shining through.

We all break and head to the quiet of our rooms for the chance of some sleep. Who knows when we will sleep again? Later in the afternoon, Matt and I head back to the markets one last time, past the ornate mosque, down through the shopping precinct with its brand-name clothes stores, electronic gadget outlets and coffee shops, skirting past the moneychangers' corner, down the narrow laneways, winding the path between workshops and storage sheds, and into the spider web of avenues that crisscross the market-place of downtown Grozny.

Here we shop for shoes and shirts, seemingly excellent quality at a fraction of the price back in Australia. For the last time we are recognised in Grozny's markets as the Australians that we are, part of Team 'Big Daddy'. Just hours before the fight, Chechen vendors reach out with their words of welcome and support.

'I wish your Lucas Browne good luck,' we hear. Sincerity coats their words. But loyalty is in their hearts: 'But I wish for Ruslan to win.'

The day is almost done when we return to the hotel, which we find buzzing with activity as boxers and their teams organise themselves and depart for the Colosseum. For some, fight night has begun. We wind our way through the crowd in the hotel foyer and try to catch the lift. There is such a demand for the elevators that we wait for more than ten minutes until we remember the service lift. We arrive on our floor to find most of our team getting ready for departure.

It is 6 pm and Lucas takes care of the mundane tasks of packing his gear for the fight. He has his two mouthguards, *his trunks, protective guard, socks and hoodie. He has packed his Team 'Big Daddy' shirt, the same one that we will all don tonight. The WBA has his gloves under guard and waiting for him at the venue. The challenger is ready to go.*

Tonight Ruslan, our accommodating and likeable driver, will himself arrive at the Colosseum Sports Hall in style. He will join us seven Australians, our three European team members, our Chechen bodyguards and our two translators, Adam and Ibby, in one of two stretch limousines. Matt Meyerhoff has arranged the transport for this evening. The contender will arrive at the venue in style, typical of Matt's support of and commitment to Lucas. He is a passionate believer in the big man, and no bandwagon jumper – he helped build the bandwagon years ago.

As we wind our way through the city streets, eager locals notice the limos, correctly guessing they have something to do with tonight's big fight. Within our car, an air of contained excitement expresses itself when the Browne boys lead us in a spine-tingling rendition of Crowded House's 'Better Be Home Soon'. And now we are here, at the Grozny Colosseum Sports Hall.

An official from the venue greets us as our car pulls into an almost deserted driveway that leads to a backdoor entrance. We are quietened by the atmosphere and the occasion, and are escorted deep into the dungeons of the Colosseum Sports Hall, to a small change room that opens out into a gym area. The room has a massage table, a table with two or three chairs, a lounge, and nothing much else. Here Lucas is much more pensive, quietly mentally preparing, but still relaxed enough to chat casually. Somehow I had imagined a grander space for a would-be heavyweight champ than this claustrophobic room. With the rest of our team, I walk out through the gym, past another gym that contains a wall-mounted television showing the bouts taking place in the arena, and we walk up two flights of stairs, the second of which delivers us into the pulsating atmosphere of the Colosseum. We stand among the crowd on this viewing platform, the ring less than twenty metres away. Lucas leans against the rails, his brothers by his side, seemingly lost in the depths of his thoughts.

In a few hours, we will be down on the floor next to that ring, taking up our privileged positions behind the blue corner, as he fights for the world title. Lanyards dangle from our necks, our invaluable passports to ringside.

The noise from the crowd is almost a physical force, such is their excitement and such are the acoustics in the Colosseum. The Sports Hall is yet another first-class facility, with the audience sitting above the ring in steeply sloped seating, either intimidating or uplifting for a boxer, depending on where the crowd's loyalty lies. We have seen enough for now and retreat to the quiet of our room, so embedded in the depths of the venue that the sound that was deafening only moments ago is barely audible.

There should still be a couple of hours before fight time, but the card is whizzing past as fight after fight finishes quickly. The small room in which Lucas sits is growing hot and stuffy, so some of us take our leave, allowing Lucas some comfort and privacy.

We walk down the hallway into the gym with the TV. We watch as the world-class South African Ali Funeka wins a split-decision victory over the Russian welterweight Viskhan Murzabekov – and the twelve rounds they fought help get the timing of the card back on track. As Funeka is grinding out his win, Lucas is in the gym outside his change room shadow-boxing, lightly limbering up, tapping Rodney's hit-pads, getting in the zone, but not overdoing it. His D-Day is upon him; within the hour, he will be in the ring, just him, Chagaev and Stanley Christodoulou.

Before we know it, the moment has arrived. An official appears at Lucas's room to lead us to a waiting room near the fighter's entrance to the arena. Lucas strides through the basement rooms of the Colosseum with Rodney, the rest of us trailing behind, our voices echoing through the concreted spaces below the stadium. The waiting room is small, but with chairs laid out for the team and a television mounted to the wall, broadcasting fellow heavyweight Brian Minto's fight just outside in the ring.

The mood is contained in the waiting room, Lucas moving around to keep warm and nimble. Minto is stopped in the second round by his heavy-punching German opponent. The time has come.

Lucas and Rodney are led to the door of the lift well, on the other side of which is a platform which will deliver them to a walkway at ring level.

Rodney leans in close. 'You are here in this place and this time for a reason,' he says. Pointing to Browne's tattoo, he continues, 'Look at what that says right there. You were born to do this.'

The official beside them holds a clipboard in his hands and speaks through his clipped-on microphone to the control room. *He then turns to Browne and Williams and in English tells them, 'It is time. Are you ready to go?'*

The doors slide open and the two take a couple of steps forward and stand on the marked spots on the platform. The noise assaults them like a physical force, a rare cocktail of Chechen cheering and the chiming of bells that opens AC/DC's 'Hell's Bells'. The glare of spotlights flashes. The gladiator emerges from below the Colosseum. The crowd wants Lucas sacrificed.

The rest of us have made our way to ringside. Our senses are struck by the electric atmosphere that confronts us. Music blares, spotlights flash and flicker, Chechen flags wave. President Kadyrov stands just on the other side of the ring to us and the crowd goes berserk. I take the time to spin around and survey the scene, soaking up the occasion. I can't believe I am here, ringside in Grozny. The seating towers above me, an amphitheatre of noise. I look back to the ring. From where I stand, just behind the blue corner, I will be an eyewitness to boxing history. Beside me is Matt Meyerhoff and to his right stand Lucas's brothers. To my left is the Frenchman, Alexandre Komurian. Soon, on the apron will be Matt, Philippe and, of course, Rodney.

Through the din, AC/DC blares, the thirteen ringing chimes that announce 'Hell's Bells'. With Rodney by his side, Lucas strides out along the walkway, reflecting the blue of the Australian flag above, bordered by glaring lights. Shooting streams of smoke complete the dramatic scene.

They step onto the white illuminated platform, Rodney clapping, Lucas sneaking a quick glance upwards, as their moving platform lowers them to ring level. Dressed in the

Team 'Big Daddy' T-shirt and the trunks emblazoned with the Australian flag, he stares resolutely ahead, arms hanging by his side. He could be the ruthless executioner – or the unaware innocent about to be dispatched.

Rodney pulls the ropes apart and Lucas steps through. He is here, the time and place have arrived. Now he can do what no Australian boxer has ever done.

I must have been lost in the moment because I now realise Chagaev is about to enter the ring. The world champion stands, hulking in his corner, the national flag of Uzbekistan proudly draped across his shoulders, ready to defend his title.

The American ring announcer, the unmistakeable Michael Buffer, has announced the fighters and now introduces the Australian national anthem. Arm in arm, we four Aussies at ringside sing 'Advance Australia Fair' with pride. We stand respectfully for the national anthem of Chagaev's native Uzbekistan, sung live in the ring as the world champion mouths along with the lyrics.

Now, the formalities gather momentum. Michael Buffer has the Chechen crowd in his hands, his silken voice ratcheting up the fervour: 'Salaam aleikum Grozny. Salaam aleikum Chechnya. Salaam aleikum Ramzan Kadyrov.'

He performs his final duty before the fight commences, introducing both boxers. We hear the familiar statistics of the man from Sydney, Australia, a perfect professional career, twenty-three fights, twenty-three victories, twenty-one knockouts. Lucas 'Big Daddy' Browne raises his right arm to salute the polite applause.

And then the two-time world champion is presented, thirty-seven professional fights, thirty-four wins, twenty-

one by knockout, two losses and one draw. The applause for Ruslan Chagaev sounds like thunder.

To the deafening roar of the crowd, Buffer declares the bout ready to begin. 'Let's get ready to rumble!'

II. Hell's Bells

The bout begins slowly. Neither the champion nor the challenger takes any unnecessary risks to start with. Browne moves lightly on his feet, circling and sizing up his opponent, while Chagaev hunts his prey. The Uzbek pushes forward, gloves held high, head moving, jabbing sharply and throwing the occasional roundhouse left. For his part Browne avoids close exchanges, throwing jabs from the back foot. If anyone was expecting a whirlwind start to this world title fight, with the challenger chancing his arm in the search to deploy his big right hand early, they soon learn otherwise. This would be a contest of a different nature.

Browne returns to his corner with his mouth dry, nerves that he hadn't been aware of taking their effect. Trainer Williams reassures him that nerves are part of the deal. 'It's a world title fight you're in, not some backyard blue,' he says, 'Start to look for opportunities. Keep the head and foot movement going. He hasn't had a real dig at you yet.'

The world is watching. Everyone sees Browne moving, up on his toes, flicking out his jab, staying out of trouble early, holding his own. His mobility and evasion are much improved, but as yet he has been unable to unload on Chagaev, whose head movement is making him an elusive target.

In these early exchanges Browne uses his feet to try to avoid Chagaev's big overhand left and attempts to find his range with his jabs. Muscle memory has taken over – feet move, head and torso sway and hips swivel. His eyes are fixed on Chagaev's, which give nothing away, not even when a heavier blow lands flush. Nothing is said between the two warriors, no trash talk, no goading, just silence.

For the next few rounds Chagaev stalks Browne, tagging him with some solid jabs and straight lefts, but, equally, Browne scores with his jabs and the odd telling right uppercut. By the end of the fourth round, there is not much in it, but the champion is ahead, due to the crispness of his punches. Browne's whole world has narrowed to that square of stretched canvas, beneath the glare and heat of television lighting. A wall of sound assaults him, its force heavy. When he lands a blow, the noise quietens, but when struck, the noise becomes a roar. Browne is friendless here. But he shuts it all out, the heat, the noise, the aloneness. His focus has narrowed to Chagaev.

The fifth round plays out like the first four, except that now some of Chagaev's blows appear to be hurting Browne. One leading right hand from the champion catches Browne on his forehead and momentarily appears to wobble him. Browne continues with his lateral movement and fires in some scoring shots of his own, sometimes leading with his right. Many of his blows however, land as counterpunches, with his weight going backwards. Chagaev has yet to taste the full power of Browne's right hand. The reigning champion certainly has the better of the exchanges in the fifth round. The champion is ahead on points – but Browne is in the contest.

III. 'Ruslan! Ruslan!'

The sixth round would prove to be the round that defines Lucas 'Big Daddy' Browne as a boxer. In the fourth and fifth, Chagaev had cranked up his aggression, perhaps impatient with Browne being a more elusive target than he had anticipated. He was managing to sneak some darting left hands through the challenger's gloves and Browne returned to his corner thinking that he was in quite a fight. Williams sent him out to meet Chagaev in the sixth with the advice 'the best defence is offence.'

The tempo lifted noticeably in the sixth round and Chagaev's snaking left hand had zeroed in and found its target. Looking sharper than it had earlier in the contest, it found its way over Browne's guard, jolting his head back with the crispness of the contact. One of those left hands caught the Australian over the left eye and he came out of the exchange with a thin line of blood trailing down his face.

Chagaev sensed that here was the moment. He poured the pressure on the challenger and now the punches started to land heavier and with more accuracy. Browne countered with a couple of solid uppercuts as his corner yelled for him to push his opponent back. But Chagaev had blood in his nostrils – and Browne was now bleeding from the cut over his left eye and from a graze high on the forehead. Some of it had smeared over the Uzbek.

With forty seconds left to go in the round, the fight took a dramatic turn. Chagaev had been hunting Browne for most of the round, his weapon of choice his missile-like left hand. But it was a swinging right that swung the contest way in favour of the champion. As he moved Browne over towards the blue corner, the Australian fired a left jab at him, opening up his ribs as a target.

Chagaev crouched down defensively and then accepted the invitation, straightening up as he looped in a power right hand that glided under Browne's elbow and cracked him in the body. Browne did not see what happened next:

> I remember bending down from the body shot, but he had set it up perfectly. I just did not see the left coming at all. His footwork was perfect and his right was a complete cover for the left.

The left hand that Chagaev landed flush on Browne's face came from a long way back. He had time to wind it up, his weight swivelling forward and Browne's going backwards. To the frantic roar of the Chechen crowd, Browne's right leg splayed outwards, his balance gone. The big man rolled onto the canvas. Referee Christodoulou hurried in and started to count. 'Get up Lucas! Get up Lucas!' came the cry from his corner.

Browne rose to his feet, looking stunned, shaking his head and trying to clear it. He is still unsure of where the blow had come from.

When Chagaev came at him again, he knew where he was, what the situation was like and how he was going, but his coordination was lagging from the big blow and Chagaev knew it. Browne's hands hung low, his defences shot. With twenty seconds left on the clock Chagaev went looking for the finishing touch, his sharp hands firing rapidly. Another wicked left connected with Browne's jaw and virtually lifted him off his feet. He was thrown back against the ropes, keeping him on his feet. The end looked only one more well-timed shot away. Somehow Browne kept moving, dodging bombs and terminal damage. He back-pedalled, in his own words 'completely in survival mode'.

The three minutes was up – but the bell had not rung. Over in the challenger's corner, Philippe Fondu was aware of what was going on and screamed, 'We're over the three minutes,' but to no avail. Maybe he couldn't be heard above the din; maybe no one wanted to hear him. The round ran at least fifteen seconds over time.

Chagaev was given ample time to finish off the Australian, but he let him slip out of his grasp. Even after the bell, he landed four big blows around Browne's head. He could be excused those late punches, so loud was the roar of the Colosseum crowd. But Browne survived and slumped onto the stool in the corner, battered and bleeding.

The drama continued in Browne's corner after the sixth. Cuts man Fondu stepped into the ring and got to work on his injuries while trainer Williams kept the mood calm. It was fortuitous that Fondu was in the ring at that moment, because the presiding medical officer for the bout, a Russian doctor, came swooping towards Browne to inspect his cut eye. Knowing that referee Christodoulou hadn't instructed him to do so, Fondu feared that the zealous doctor was going to seize the moment and order the fight over. The multilingual Belgian growled at him in Russian and didn't mince his words. He told the doctor to 'fuck off, fuck off now', and that he did.

Meanwhile, Williams was more concerned about the heavy right hand that Browne had taken to the ribs than the left that put him down or the cut eye that he suffered.

'It was a flash knock down. I wasn't too worried about it, he just caught Lucas square,' Williams explained later. 'I think the right rip to the body hurt him a lot more than the left to the head. And the cut, well he gets cut in every fight.'

In the ring Fondu looked in his fighter's eyes and asked, 'Are you okay?' He got no answer. While he attended to the cut, Fondu tried again to assess Browne's condition. 'Is it okay?' he asked the boxer again.

This time Lucas Browne responded, 'Well it better be.'

Browne's mind was clearing, but he still had the feeling that his body wasn't receiving clear signals from his brain. The crowd smelled blood in the water and were going berserk. President Kadyrov was on his feet, waving his arms, pumping up the red corner, yelling his support for Chagaev. 'Ruslan! Ruslan!' reverberated around the amphitheatre. The noise was deafening. Amid that maelstrom of emotions, Williams knew the time had come to play the best card in his deck. Leaning in closer to his charge, he knew that pride was the key. 'Do you want your family to see you go out this way?' he asked. 'Is this what you want them to see?' And then pointing to his right glove and then to his left, he said, 'These are your boys. This is Billy and this is Isaac. Now go out there and get the job done.'

What the audience at ringside and those watching around the world then witnessed was stunning. Just a minute before, Browne seemed out on his feet, just one more big shot away from oblivion. Now in the seventh, he made a stand, valiantly trying to change roles from helpless prey to marauding predator.

Browne saw things this way:

It shows your true self. I honestly don't think you know who you truly are until you're in a situation like that, in the ring or not. Some people would back off, but no, not me, I'm going forward.

Browne took the fight to Chagaev at a time when Chagaev expected him to be weakened and retreating. His counterattack was brutal and unsophisticated, landing a series of thundering uppercuts and overhand rights. But each time he launched his uppercuts, he opened up his head to Chagaev's sniping lefts and the champion obliged. The exchanges were heavy at times, but Browne's unexpected offensive had succeeded in winning a reprieve from Chagaev's onslaught. In the seventh, Browne won a battle, but not yet the war. With Browne in the ascendancy, the round concluded early, with forty-four seconds still on the clock, another inexplicable error in timing.

The tide must have turned in the fortunes of the fight for, during the break, President Kadyrov climbed up to ringside and had his hand through the ropes, massaging his fighter's neck and giving him encouragement. A clear rule limited the support team to three on the apron of the ring and Christodoulou moved across and instructed the president to move away.

The South African ref had been half expecting President Kadyrov's fervour to get the better of him and was ready for just this eventuality:

I had seen Mr Kadyrov do that exact thing on a previous trip there so when he did it, I was mentally prepared. Admittedly, I was probably more polite to him than I would have been to some person who wasn't as important, but all I said to him was 'Mr President, please'. Fortunately he responded by leaving the apron.'

Both boxers had spent a lot of energy in those frantic two rounds and, in the eighth and ninth, the pace dropped. Chagaev and Browne looked fatigued, the Australian's hands dropping lower, his face bloodied from the hammering he took in the sixth round. But Browne was moving forward more than he had earlier in the fight and was still flicking his jab out. That being said, the champion had started to claw his way back on top with crisper shots as the bell sounded to conclude the ninth.

As Ruslan Chagaev stood to answer the bell for the tenth, his trainer, Pedro Diaz, spoke forcefully to him, with their faces close together, pumping him up for a final assault. Chagaev stood, and fighter and trainer slapped hands together. He went out to meet Browne for what would prove to be the final round.

IV. The Punch

Most of the tenth round never even hinted at the drama that was to come. Browne moved backwards for most of the round, his jab keeping the champion at bay. The fight seemed to be running out of steam and heading towards a points win to Chagaev. Then, with just under a minute to go in the round, he manoeuvred Browne over towards the Australian's blue corner.

As Chagaev moved forward he threw another big left that slid over Browne's head and across his left shoulder as he ducked to avoid it. He had left his head open to Browne's best punch, his thunderous right. Coming up from his crouched defensive stance, Browne was like a tightened spring uncoiling.

Browne threw the most sweetly timed punch of the fight. As he stood up from his bent position, he let loose a huge roundhouse right that caught Chagaev flush under his left ear, sending him staggering backwards. In that dramatic moment the fortunes of the fight changed hands.

The champion, who had been pushing forward for much of this tenth round and, indeed, for most of the contest, was suddenly teetering backwards. Browne pursued him, right fist cocked, as Chagaev lost his battle to keep his balance and collapsed backwards, rolling over onto his right shoulder.

Referee Christodoulou jumped in and, for the second time in the fight, applied a standing eight count. All the while, Browne stood in the neutral corner, his face bashed and bloodied, and waited, listening to a small number of Australian accents over in his blue corner going ballistic. Despite the hysteria and adrenaline surge, he clearly heard the voice of his manager, Matt Clark, the advice simple: 'Jump on him, Lucas, jump on him.'

Chagaev was patently dazed and disorientated. When Christodoulou signalled fight on, Browne knew he had a vulnerable and badly wounded target. He virtually ran across the ring to take advantage of the doorway that had opened for him. He shoved his way through it.

The wounded champion had leaned back against the ropes near the red corner, which meant Browne had him where he wanted him. To the manic screams of his team – 'Go for him, Lucas! Smash him, Lucas!' – Browne trapped Chagaev against the ropes near the red corner and took to him with ferocious power. He fired four, five, six, seven murderous right hands. In a relentless series of thunderous rights, Browne herded and bashed Chagaev around past the corner and further along the ropes, until he struck him with some lefts that had him back to where the mauling commenced. Browne had thrown fourteen or fifteen vicious blows, most of them finding Chagaev's head. The stadium had gone strangely quiet, but those in the challenger's corner didn't notice it because they were roaring, scarcely believing what was unfolding before our eyes. Chagaev did his best to protect himself, but was unable to respond with a single punch. Yet he stayed on his feet under the withering assault, courageous, proud champion that he was.

Chagaev is defenceless against big lefts, big rights. Browne is throwing heavy blows at will and receiving nothing in return. Stanley Christodoulou steps in, arms spread wide to protect Chagaev. The contest is over.

V. Gronzy Chronicle – Continued

We can't believe it. Lucas 'Big Daddy' Browne has gotten up off the canvas, bloodied and bruised, refusing to wilt, creating a story for the ages. He raises his arm in triumph.

Ringside, we are ecstatic, screaming, hugging and fist-waving. His manager, Matt, hurdles over the top rope into the ring, embracing the new WBA world champion. I am on the apron of the ring, but just as I am about to slip through the ropes and join the celebration inside the ring, everything changes.

Michael Buffer is now back in the ring, announcing what most boxing fans never expected to hear: 'A new heavyweight champion of the world, from Australia, still undefeated, Lucas "Big Daddy" Browne.' It's what the crowd did not want to hear.

A change has swept through the Colosseum. As WBA official Renzo Bagnariol holds the new champion's arm aloft in triumph, the crowd boos. President Kadyrov looks displeased. Browne consoles Chagaev, who also seems upset with the referee's call. Browne goes to shake the hand of one of Chagaev's cornermen – who turns his back. The mood has turned black. There will be no victory speech for the Australian. The new world champion is led immediately from the ring by his team. This is no place for triumphant celebrations. Browne's three armed bodyguards sweep into action, getting him out of there. Getting him to safety.

Everything had changed – and it would soon all change again.

Siylah Lucas

I. Grozny Chronicle – Saturday night, Sunday morning, 5–6 March 2016

In this moment of triumph, the crowd is silent. It's as if there has been a death. President Kadyrov is waving his arms in frustration, stroking his beard, clearly upset at the result. He abruptly departs the arena.

This seems to be the signal for a mass exit, just as Chagaev is giving a speech in defeat. There is no opportunity for a dignified victory speech, to acknowledge Chagaev's reign or to savour the moment. This is not a moment for glory – just an emptying arena, a darkening venue, a telecast cut short and an overwhelming mood of despair. Lucas and Danny sense the change in mood immediately. Danny is suddenly the big brother, protector and leader of our team, telling us urgently to bottle our joy, settle now, be dignified.

There are concerns for Lucas's safety. We gather ourselves and our equipment and retreat as quickly as we can into the sheds.

Now Lucas sits in the change room, composed, quietly talking, assessing his injuries. His left eye needs stitching, abrasions to his forehead and small swellings to the sides of his head require attention. I can now see up close what a wonderful job Philippe Fondu has done to nurse Lucas's cuts through the latter rounds. Because of his expertise they were hardly an issue but, now I can see the extent of them, I wonder how they weren't.

Lucas's left kidney aches where Chagaev connected twice. But the injury that upsets Lucas the most is his lost implant from a tooth. No-one, not even a world heavyweight champion like Lucas Browne, enjoys being punched.

Had I pictured this moment before tonight, I would have imagined a euphoric change room, one carried away by emotion, jubilation at the new champion's achievement. This is nothing like that. Had I entertained the thought of defeat, this is more the atmosphere I would have assigned to it. The reception and reaction to Chagaev's defeat have stolen our celebration of the moment – but not all of it. Lucas sits back with the world title belt draped across his chest in satisfaction, a broad grin coming to his face. His strapping is cut from his hands and he changes into his grey tracksuit and pulls a beanie down low, covering the abrasion to his forehead.

A Russian television crew appears outside the room requesting an interview with the new world champion. Their initial question captures the spirit of the moment for Lucas. He is asked how he feels about the fight, about winning the world title. Lucas probably surprises them with his answer:

Obviously I'm not very pleased with some aspects of the fight. As you can see I took a bit of punishment. But of course I'm happy with the way it turned out.

If they are expecting an exuberant showman trumpeting his achievements, they don't get one. Lucas speaks quietly, respectfully and thoughtfully.

A Chechen official arrives at our change room door to escort Lucas for post-fight drug testing, again to be conducted by VADA. Rodney and Matt, along with our Chechen bodyguards and translators, accompany Lucas to a gym area, where he is to wait while a sample is taken from Chagaev first.

Meanwhile the rest of us sit or lie around on gym mats, in conversation or thought. I sit with Danny and Pat as well as American fighter Brian Minto. The talk is all brotherly pride, as you would expect.

In the now early hours of Sunday morning, the venue feels deserted, our voices echoing through our subterranean bunker, the roar of the crowd long gone.

After more than an hour, the new champion, his trainer and his manager return. Apparently Chagaev had been dehydrated and had difficulty providing a sample.

We leave the stadium in the waiting limousine and it ghosts its way through the deserted, silent streets of inner-city Grozny, the cabin of the car muffling the triumphant singing of Queen's 'We Are the Champions'.

Unlike the empty cityscape through which we have just passed, the foyer of the Grozny City Hotel is alive with excitement and well-wishers. Lucas is swamped by other *fighters and their teams, hotel staff, officials and some invited guests. It is his very first taste of the spoils of victory, but he is not too keen on savouring it; he prefers to retreat to the privacy of our twenty-fourth floor.*

There we sit, enjoying the moment, eating chicken, watching the night sky give way to the approaching dawn in Grozny, downing a few quiet, celebratory beers. By 5 am the champion needs his sleep. Rodney, Pat, Matt and I venture back down to the ground floor and out into the early morning chill, where we share a Cuban cigar, savouring the last remaining moments of this momentous day. Before we sleep, we soak up all the joy we can from the dawn over Grozny.

II. What the World Saw

'I went into this fight like I go into every fight, thinking I'm going to be fine, I'm the man,' says Lucas Browne, looking back at his moment of glory. 'At that first break I thought, "Wow, I'm actually in a fight, this is legit." I knew I had a battle on my hands.' Rodney Williams whispered wise words of counsel in his ear at that moment. They did the trick.

Fourteen thousand kilometres away in the north-western Sydney suburb of Baulkham Hills, a very proud mother, Leonie Browne, sat in her lounge room on this early Sunday morning, in the company of some of her grandchildren. On edge and nervous, Leonie couldn't relax. She took up position in front of the telecast sitting on a footstool. When she saw her son emerge onto the platform before the fight, nerves gave way to pride:

I was just so proud at that moment. You're a parent and you see your son and ask yourself if it's really him doing this. I didn't actually break into tears until I saw him singing the national anthem.

Her son's thoughts at the time were a little different: 'Shit, is this thing going to hold my weight?' and then, 'Do not fall.' It did; he didn't.

Browne stuck to the plan in his fight, never losing focus. It was only after the fight was done that he recognised some of the thoughts that had flitted through his mind in the ring. At one moment, in those first four or five rounds, as he glided around the ring, he was considering what fans back home were thinking about his performance and, in particular, about his foot movement and style. Having allowed himself that momentary luxury of concentration, Browne was once again back in the here and now, in a state of heightened alert, thinking about where he should be in relation to Chagaev:

He would want me to sit in the pocket and trade with him. I didn't want to, it was the last thing I intended to do. He was very sharp and very strong and when he was hitting me, I could feel his power. So I kept moving.

He recalls the knockdown in the sixth round that had him in trouble. 'I thought, "Shit, that's not good. Better get up. Okay I'm up; I'm here but not really here.'"

Back home, Browne's mum thought to herself:

Oh he's so tough. I just want him to get to the end of
the twelve rounds, but if he doesn't win, he's got there.
What he's achieved is amazing. Either way, win or lose,
I am so proud.

In the ring, Stanley Christodoulou had the best view of
the blows that put Browne on the canvas. He describes the
knockdown as 'pretty routine'. The vastly experienced referee
had no concerns for the Australian's immediate welfare:

He was a little stunned, but crucially, the muscle tone in
his neck was fine; that's a clear sign of when a boxer is
in distress and unable to defend himself properly.

So Christodoulou had no hesitation applying the standing
eight count and letting the fight to continue.

The knockdown was not going to cost Browne the fight –
but he knew that what immediately followed might:

The worst thing that Chagaev ever did was to allow me
to recover in that sixth round. If he had jumped on me
and kept going, bullied me and pushed me around, I
would have been gone.

Maybe a younger, more assertive Ruslan Chagaev would
have seized the moment, but the fact remained that Browne's
counterattack in the seventh successfully held off the Uzbek.

It was a different matter altogether when Browne went
after Chagaev once the Uzbek got himself up off the canvas
in the tenth round. This time Christodoulou saw a dazed and

badly hurt fighter, struggling to defend himself, unable to respond, taking a terrible flogging.

In his view, there was only one possible action that he could take:

> Chagaev had been dropped and got up in time, but
> when Browne attacked, he was pinned on the ropes
> and was offering nothing. It wasn't just that he wasn't
> throwing punches back, but he wasn't even trying to slip
> the blows. Chagaev was taking a pounding and, in my
> opinion, he was one or two punches away from being
> seriously hurt and my job in the ring is to protect the
> boxers.

The decision to step between the fighters – just as another heavy shot landed on Chagaev's left ear – and signal the fight over was not a difficult one.

Over in the blue corner, Philippe Fondu, the boxing journeyman who has seen it all, thought he could be about to witness a death in the ring.

'He was hitting him with many big shots. Chagaev was defenceless at the time,' he says. 'If Stanley didn't stop it when he did, I'm worried that Lucas would have killed him.'

With typical understatement, Browne recalls the punch that set up his victory:

> The punch came back to instinct and muscle memory.
> We had trained for Chagaev to open up later in the
> fight after hooking with his left. I just saw his head
> and threw it. It is one of my favourite punches, half an

uppercut and half a hook. My timing has always been spot on and my reactions always sharp, so, at the time, I didn't think anything, I just did it.

Browne's assault on Chagaev from that point wasn't technically pretty, but it was effective. 'Big Daddy' describes it this way:

> It was my time to capitalise. I've got the size and the reach to swamp anyone and I knew I had him. It was random everything, but they were all heavy punches and he couldn't recover. Some of the ones he took on the gloves were still hitting him around the temple area.

Browne was about to apply the finishing touch.

> I was thinking everything is arm punches, so I was about to step back from him and get the distance to really put the weight of my body behind the next punch. I think it would have hurt him properly and that's exactly what I wanted to do at that point.

He knew what he was about to do – which is why he agrees that Christodoulou made the right decision. 'The timing of the stoppage was great.'

As soon as the referee stepped in, Browne moved away from the stricken Chagaev and raised both arms in a victory salute. But he wasn't carried away by the historic nature of what he had just achieved:

It wasn't for the fact that I'd won a world title, but just that it was over. None of the title idea sank in; it was that I had won *this* fight. I'd had to come off the canvas to do it.'

In front of the television in her lounge room, Leonie Browne just felt overwhelming pride. 'My granddaughter ran over to me and embraced me and I just sobbed and sobbed. So much so I missed what happened over the next few minutes.' Gloves off, Browne went over to the blue corner and shook hands with Pedro Diaz and put his arm around Chagaev. Across the barrier of language, Browne felt that the two fighters understood each other:

I thanked him for the fight and told him he was a great fighter. I said that it was a tough fight for me from the way he was hitting me. From his gestures and tone he didn't seem to think that it was a very good stoppage. I said that I was sorry, but it was the referee's call. I went to shake hands with someone else in his corner, but he just turned away from me.

That signalled the change of mood in the Colosseum. The new world champion was led immediately from the ring by his team. Celebrations seemed inappropriate; worse, they could enrage an angry crowd. Browne's three armed bodyguards got their man through the crowd, out of the main arena and into safety. The rest of team 'Big Daddy' trailed behind and the stair wells of the inner area of the Colosseum reverberated with a defiant 'Aussie, Aussie, Aussie! Oi, Oi, Oi!'

In the change room on the basement floor of the complex, Browne's mood was subdued. In the more private seclusion of his room, he allowed himself to sit in an appropriately throne-like chair and let the excitement of others wash past him. His adrenaline wave had crashed and the pain of his battle scars began to register.

Browne remembers the course of events well.

When I won the fight, the crowd had gone completely quiet. I looked over at the president and he's had the shits well and truly. My bodyguards had the guns so I needed them at that point and they got me through the crowd to the sheds. So now the fight's over, I've had an adrenaline dump and I feel just flat. I'm very, very sore. And the tooth, that annoyed me the most, two fights in a row and two teeth fall out. I thought about how I was going to smile for all those cameras with no tooth.

There were times when Browne thought that he was never meant to win the fight. The championship belt he wore around his neck in the ring belonged to Chagaev – having defended the title more than once, he gets to keep the belt for good. But there was no belt for Lucas Browne. After his victory, he was told that one would be sent to him within two weeks. It has never arrived.

'I was never there to win it,' Browne felt. 'They never thought I had enough in me to knock him out so it was always going to go to a points decision and I was going to lose that.'

But Lucas 'Big Daddy' Browne had risen from a mid-fight battering and persevered in a courageous back-to-the-wall victory, a display of grit and self-belief that impressed the boxing world. He had conquered Ruslan Chagaev and was now the WBA regular champion of the world, the first Australian to claim a slice of the heavyweight title in boxing history.

The fight was beamed into Australian lounge rooms by pay-per-view, the telecast commencing on Sunday morning at 6 am on the east coast. The hearts of many Australian boxing fans – and indeed his adopted British followers – swelled with pride that morning at what they had witnessed. Irrespective of where they sat on the Lucas Browne appreciation spectrum, sports fans recognise an audacious against-the-odds performance when they see one.

One such fan was trainer Johnny Lewis, who had seen so many courageous displays over his long, distinguished career in the boxing game. You don't train the likes of Jeff Fenech, Kostya Tszyu and Jeff 'Hitman' Harding without being a close witness to inspiring acts of fortitude. But what this great trainer who has seen it all saw in Grozny stirred his admiration:

I felt very proud for a good young man who went
against the odds. He didn't have much in his favour at
all. In that boxing ring it's very hard to pick yourself up
off the canvas and not just win but win by knockout,
like he did. It speaks volumes for his courage. His
determination to win the fight was of the highest level.
He kept on backing himself no matter what. I thought

he was behind on points, but he believed in himself throughout. Self-belief got him over the line.

As well as self-belief and courage, Lewis alludes to a quality that is less definable, a trait that sometimes determines success or failure.

'You wouldn't have thought he'd get through that sixth round,' Lewis remembers. 'He drew on something very, very special. It is something that comes from within. It's got to do with mental toughness and his was superb.'

Commentator Ben Damon saw the fight in a similar light.

The dream of any boxer is to win against the odds. And there are no greater odds than to be away from home, to be friendless in the venue, to be knocked down and seemingly be out of the contest and then to get up off the canvas and stop your opponent. That's the stuff of heroes.

As events were destined to play out in the months ahead, Browne would need that mental toughness in bucket loads. If the rollercoaster of boxing had taken Lucas 'Big Daddy' Browne to dizzying heights, it was about to take him to a new low. The power from within that had helped him prevail in that ring in Grozny would be sorely needed in the battle that was to come.

For as he waited to be tested by the VADA officials in the early hours of that Sunday morning, minute traces of the banned substance clenbuterol coursed through his body.

CHAPTER TEN

The World Champion That Never Was

I. Grozny Chronicle – Sunday, 6 March 2016

I have slept for no more than an hour, and I'm not sure what has woken me after so little sleep. Bleary-eyed and hazy-minded, I take in my surroundings, the familiar Grozny hotel room bringing me back to reality. The magnitude of the events of the past few hours hits me. A quick reality check: yes, that all really did happen; Lucas Browne is the WBA regular heavyweight champion of the world. As I lie there in my bed, I enjoy the solitude and the opportunity to savour Lucas's feat, before the outside world encroaches.

I wonder what is happening back home, how his victory is being received and reported. Australia loves a winner, especially one who has beaten the odds. It is early afternoon on the east coast of the country and I imagine the television networks would be beating the hell out of this amazing Rocky-style victory. If Lucas was not a major identity on the Australian sporting landscape before, that is all about to change. But here in Grozny, it is just after nine in the morning and I can hear excited voices coming from around the corner of the hallway.

I go to bid good morning to the bodyguard stationed outside my room, but there is no one there. The seat, for the first time since I arrived, is unoccupied. With the title now won by the invader, perhaps security is no longer a priority? But I am deceived – it is just a change in shift and, soon enough, another armed Chechen hovers near the new world champion. Whoever should wish Lucas Browne harm here in Grozny just missed their chance. Or maybe not.

I find Matt Clark and Rodney in Lucas's room. Unlike three or four hours ago, the big man is now buzzing with excitement. The brutal reality of a tough fight had hold of him last night, leaving him bloodied, bruised and missing a tooth. The potentially life-changing nature of his achievement had yet to settle upon him. The only euphoria I witnessed from Lucas was in the seconds after Stanley Christodoulou stepped in to protect Chagaev. Lucas stood, the result sealed, with his arms raised above his head. That he had to retreat from the ring and slink his way back to the change rooms like a criminal was not at all befitting a world champion. It burns a little. But it was what it was and nothing can change that. Lucas was sombre after the fight, but now his wide smile and glowing eyes are those of a man allowing himself the luxury of contemplating his achievements. Here in room 2309 in the Grozny City Hotel sits the WBA regular heavyweight champion of the world and he has six gold medallions to prove it. Each medallion sits comfortably in its own green felt–lined box, emblazoned with the seal *of the WBA, encircled by the details of the fight: 'Ruslan Chagaev Vs Lucas Browne Grozny March 5th 2016'. On the reverse side is the symbol for the Akhmat Fight Club. The medallions have been delivered to Lucas by Alex Fedesov, the good-natured Russian who has so professionally ensured the smooth conduct of the whole event.*

The medallions are no substitute for the title belt, but are a tangible proof of his triumph nevertheless. More important than the medallions was the knock at his door that woke Lucas just after eight this morning. Lucas, groggy from lack of sleep and the toll that the fight exacted, staggered to answer the door. He found standing in front of him none other than Kostya Tszyu.

The four-time world champion, an inductee into the International Boxing Hall of Fame, had come to pay his respects, one champion to another. Kostya and Lucas spoke about the fight and what may now lie ahead for Lucas. Kostya offered two things to Lucas: his full support in any way he could give it and the simple advice that Lucas now had to work a lot harder again, now he had become the hunted and not the hunter. Kostya had not long left when I entered the room.

Soon enough we are all in the room, our Team 'Big Daddy', the man himself, his trainer, Rodney Williams, his manager, Matt Clark, his brothers, Danny and Patrick, his mate Matt Meyerhoff, and myself. We are back sitting around Lucas's room, like we had just a few hours before and like we have numerous times during the week, but it's all different now: the tension is gone, the job is complete – Lucas Browne has done what he set out to do. The room is messed with the leftover meals from a few hours before, the stale smell of fried chicken heavy in the air. Nine or ten empty bottles stand forlornly on the small desk and the bedside table. None would have Lucas's fingerprints on them; he celebrated with a can of Pepsi.

Some of us scan Facebook or other social media and report that the impact back in Australia seems huge. Others just sit and smile, soaking up the heady atmosphere of being a small cog in this world championship–winning machine. We are all booked on the Russian Red Wings flight departing at 3.15 pm and now, at about 11 am, our mission in Grozny is drawing to a close. We all retreat to our rooms and pack, gathering again in the hotel foyer. Here Lucas is the centre of attention; fellow boxers, their entourages, hotel staff and random hotel guests are lining up for photos with the champion. There is a virtual sea of well-wishers.

Boxing is renowned for the backslapper; it is the sport where everyone wants a piece of the winner before he becomes the loser, but I can't help thinking that this man has left quite an impression on those who have met him here. We shuffle through the crowded lobby, out through the revolving doors into the vestibule, past the seated guards and out the door to the fresh air outside. Here, for the final time, awaits Ruslan with his van, ready for our departure to the airport.

The seven of us jump on board, together with our now two good friends, Adam and Ibby. They have been more than translators; they have been troubleshooters and problem-solvers; they have been confidants and advisers; they have been the conduit connecting our Australian ways with Chechen customs, and they have most certainly *been minders, guiding us through minefields of cultural complexities and social expectations. Along the way, they both became part of the Lucas Browne team. The mood in the bus is jubilant as we retrace our route back out from the city centre, past the shops and arcades that so bemused me just a week ago, out into the suburbs where the road is wide and the rendered dwellings sit low and sprawling. Like Australian homes, many have front yards and backyards, but not many have dividing fences shutting out their neighbours. Perhaps they have a different view about community than we in the West. Or perhaps when you are rebuilding a shattered city, one flattened by the fist of oppression, a fence is not a high priority.*

As we drive on, song, laughter and shouting fill the van. Suddenly, Lucas calls for Ruslan to stop the van and, when he pulls over, in front of us stands a huge billboard, belatedly advertising the showdown between our man and the one who had been champion just the day before. This billboard is different; it is the only one in Grozny in English.

At least 6 metres tall and 4 metres wide, elevated another two metres or so on its metal legs, the billboard has a meaning it did not have yesterday. Now, when its very message has been rendered obsolete, the billboard assumes almost iconic significance to us, capturing forever this moment in time.

Lucas hurries over to the cemented base of the billboard's foundations and stands with his arms raised in the V of victory. All of us gather beside him, a team proud of their man, a team that feels it has ventured far off the beaten track and achieved a dream. Fists pumping amid shouts of delight, a chant of 'Siylah Lucas' starts up. Across the wide road, lanes separated by a tree-lined island, is a sports field. Although none of us has noticed them, a band of twenty or so boys playing there, about ten to twelve years old, have seen us. They brave the traffic and storm across to us, all of them seemingly recognising the new world champion.

If we didn't appreciate it before, we certainly see now how large this fight has loomed in Grozny. Lucas stays on the platform below the billboard, but the rest of us leave the stage for the Chechen boys to have their moment with the champ. They swarm around him, chattering and smiling broadly, their photos being taken with the man who towers above them.

Lucas indulges them; these boys will have a story to tell in the years ahead, of how they met the Australian world champ. The cynic in me suggests he is new to this fame, that, given enough time, he will tire of it and become insular like so many successful sports stars – but that's only the cynic; the rest of me does not think so. Lucas is genuine; he takes a moment for these boys because it is the right thing to do. As we bid goodbye, we turn to make our way back to the van, but our attention is drawn back to the boys. They stand together in a tight knot, facing us, their fists pumping the air above their heads, joined in one voice, their faces strained with emotion, their chant simple, but humbling, 'Siylah Lucas! Siylah Lucas!', 'Lucas the Great! Lucas the Great!' After all that has occurred this week, through all the drama and intrigue, the friendship and the challenges, the danger and the risk, these boys' respect for Lucas is the icing on the cake. But just as we board the van, one dissenting child's voice can be detected in the chorus of adoration. That voice is singing 'Siylah Ruslan!' That too makes us smile.

Grozny airport. It was the first target of the Russian assault in the second war with Chechnya. It was flattened. Now it is much like an Australian provincial airport, large enough but still with the simple feel of days gone by.

Its arrival lounge feels like a large airy hangar on cemented floors. As passengers arrive, they collect their luggage by being funnelled into an adjacent room no larger than a small school classroom, where they jostle and weave their way through the milling crowd. Now in the departure lounge, we have farewelled and thanked Adam, Ibby and Ruslan, these humble, smiling men, who have guided us. All the seats are occupied, so our team gathers in a corner near a souvenir shop. Soon, other passengers gather around Lucas and Rodney, fellow fighters who are making their way home. And there is referee Stanley Christodoulou and contest supervisor Renzo Bagnariol, who join us in conversation.

Stanley reveals that his decision to step in and stop the fight last night was one of the easiest decisions that he has been called on to make in his career. Chagaev, in his opinion, was unable to defend himself, so there was only one decision that could be made. Even if the president disagreed.

Renzo confides to Lucas that the scorecard was dire when he landed the crucial blow. Not only was he behind on all three scorecards, he was so far behind that only one result could swing the fight the Australian's way by the time the tenth round commenced. And Lucas produced that result. Judges Laine and Cova had Chagaev ahead by six points, 88 to 82, and Prayadsab scored the contest 88 to 81. Lucas had always said, long before he left Australian shores, that he was taking his own judges with him, his left and his right. And as it turned out, he needed them to take the title.

The Red Wings flight taxies towards its take-off strip, our team spreads out through economy and business class and as we fly to Moscow we have a quiet two hours alone to reflect on the past week. As our flight soars off the tarmac and banks for its flight path, from my window seat I am afforded an uninterrupted view of Grozny below. The proud spires of the cluster of buildings of which Grozny City Hotel is the focal point stand out in the cityscape. I also look beyond and view the circular structures of the Colosseum Sports Hall and I can clearly make out the crowded canvas-topped alleyways of the market.

I know with absolute certainty that Grozny is going to stay with me, like a place from a dream, ethereally mysterious and elusive, yet at the same time vividly real and tangible. This city will revisit and haunt me in the days, weeks, even years to come. I know it won't let go easily. Its people, its history, its atmosphere and the events that it has hosted have cast a spell on me. When our plane doors open, we alight onto an icy tarmac, night soon descending upon a frigid Moscow. Most passengers are funnelled towards a waiting bus for transport to the arrivals lounge, but, once out of the plane, we are met and greeted by Kostya Tszyu.

This time Lucas doesn't have the great man to himself. The chilling Moscow evening has lost its grip on us as we stand on the tarmac talking with Kostya, photos snapping and hands being shaken. Kostya directs us onto a van that *takes us to the arrivals lounge, but through a more secluded section where my passport is not required. Again, Kostya turns to Lucas and looks him in the eye.*

'Now you must work harder,' he advises, as he did this morning. 'If before you did one hundred push-ups, now you do two hundred. If before you ran for an hour, now you run for two hours.'

Kostya's message is as simple as it is demanding: others will now train harder to defeat you, so you must now work harder to defeat them. It is how a champion thinks. We are flying on to Dubai, but Kostya is travelling no further, and so we say our farewells.

We find a place that we think may provide us some privacy, a small bar and restaurant, down a side avenue of the sprawling airport. We have nearly seven hours before our departure to Dubai and some of us have been looking forward to our first real celebratory beers. So we pull up a table and make ourselves inconspicuous. No we don't – Lucas Browne is not inconspicuous, with his shaved head, huge frame and tattooed body. Soon enough, word spreads in the airport that the new heavyweight champion of the world is here and Lucas has the first of many, many requests for a photo. Not a single request is in English, but Lucas obliges each and every one of them, a glowing smile to make each photo special. A Russian security officer circles like a shark, either dubious about the situation or plucking up the courage to ask for a photo. Turns out it's the latter, for he swoops in upon Lucas at the next opportunity, handing his phone to Rodney, signalling for him to take a photo. But now he must pay the price for his hesitation – Lucas puts one arm around him as he does in all photos, but, with his left, he removes the officer's hat and places it on his own head. The officer momentarily looks bemused, but smiles broadly and he has his photo.

Two things occur to me as I sit witnessing these small and seemingly insignificant events. Firstly, the reaction of these Russian, Eastern European and Asiatic fight fans highlights the fame in this part of the world that Lucas has already attained in the immediate aftermath of his victory. This fight was no small business here and, in overcoming Ruslan Chagaev, he has stamped himself as a major player in world boxing. These people are genuinely delighted to have met him. One young woman stood, mouth agape in awe, when Lucas stepped aside for her when going through a turnstile. Secondly, in this age of insular, pampered, self-absorbed sport superstars, here is a man who genuinely enjoys his interactions with the public.

Now the challenge is over and here in Moscow we talk quietly among ourselves, about the fight, about Chagaev, about President Kadyrov and about Grozny. One of us has heard that Tyrone Spong was followed into the change room after his bout and told by a government official that President Kadyrov liked his boots and wished to have them. According to the story, Spong was told, 'Can I have them now please? Or even better, you take them off and take them to President Kadyrov and give them to him.' Another story doing the rounds is more serious. One of the judges in the bout between Ali Funeka and Viskhan Murzabekov is said to have been approached at the end of the twelfth round and instructed to change his scores. The judge stood *his ground; the result remained a split-decision victory to Funeka. Nevertheless, it does give pause for thought.*

After all the chitchat, all the speculation, all the reminiscing, one thing remains: Lucas has gone to the Chechen city and defeated the man who had only been beaten by the formidable Alexander Povetkin and the superstar Wladimir Klitschko. Consequently Lucas is now the WBA regular heavyweight champion of the world. The words taste sweet rolling off the tongue. Like Adam Scott overcoming the Australian hoodoo in the US Masters with his memorable victory at Augusta in 2013, like Cathy Freeman's 400-metre gold medal at the Sydney Olympics, Lucas Browne has smashed through the barriers of his nation's sport history. He has done it in heroic fashion, unheralded and underrated, well behind on the scorecards but refusing to wilt, climbing up off the canvas to prevail in the most extraordinary of settings. We have been witnesses to an epochal event.

Lucas will return home to a hero's welcome. In Dubai, our Team 'Big Daddy' will disband, each of us flying variously to Sydney, Perth or Brisbane. Our thoughts have drifted ahead to Lucas's first defence of his title, a possible meeting with Fres Oquendo in Australia. But, for now, Lucas needs to find the time and opportunity to savour the taste of victory, an indulgence denied him in Grozny.

The seven of us have shared an extraordinary story, an experience that comes once in a lifetime. Irrespective of what happens in the future, no matter how short or long Lucas reigns as the champion, he will always be the man who claimed the heavyweight title of the world from Ruslan Chagaev in Grozny.

II. Saint Patrick's Day

Not long after returning to Australia, Matt and I were travelling again. Of all days, we land in Dublin on the morning of Saint Patrick's Day. And of all years, we arrive in 2016 – the centenary of the Easter Rising rebellion, the landmark event in the Irish people's struggle for independence, an event of historical and, we anticipated, celebratory significance. It was a father-and-son trip that we had planned together for years, long before Lucas Browne entered our lives.

There we were in O'Connell Street, outside the GPO, which was the epicentre of the rebellion, squeezed in among half a million people, an ocean of laughing, cheering revellers bedecked in green. Less than two weeks after the events in Grozny, I was still euphoric, still riding a wave of adrenaline from the adventure of my lifetime. We wound our way across the Liffey past Temple Bar, up onto Dame Street, the long arterial road along which businesses, street vendors and restaurants thrive.

We arrived at Peadar Kearney's, a pub that borrows its name from the former Irish republican and composer of the Irish national anthem, 'The Soldier's Song'. Like so many of its kind, Peadar Kearney's oozes atmosphere and bonhomie, with its eccentric nooks and crannies, its photos and memorabilia from days long gone and the heady scent of fresh, freely flowing Guinness. We settled in, joined by some Irish friends of Matt's and some locals who, until then, were strangers to us.

Late afternoon became evening and a musician, a big man with a shaved head and a guitar, took to the small stage squeezed into the upstairs lounge. He began to sing and his huge, powerful voice filled the room. Brian Brody commanded the attention of the few hundred listeners, his guitar and his voice his only tools. He sang songs of Dublin, ballads of love, lust and drunkenness, and he had everyone clapping and dancing. After more than two hours playing there was a break in his set and, whether it was the Guinness or my adrenaline talking, I found myself in conversation with the singer. I told him where we had just been, I told him of our experiences and I told him that Matt now managed the WBA regular heavyweight champion of the world, Australia's very first.

'And you say his name is Lucas Browne? Is there some Irish in there somewhere?' Brian asked in his lilting Dublin brogue.

'Absolutely,' I responded with a certainty born of the Guinness and not factual knowledge.

Brian Brody summoned the audience's attention and, motioning at Matt and myself, announced:

'We have two Aussies here tonight and they have just come from Grozny in Chechnya. Their boxer Lucas Browne is now the world heavyweight champ.'

Without prompting, the crowd there in Peadar Kearney's, in Dublin on the far side of the world to Australia, began punching the air in acknowledgement and chanting 'Lucas Browne' over and over again. And then Brian Brody's guitar again became the centre of attention, his introduction, like a sorcerer's wand, weaving its spell of magic and settling silence upon the crowd until the guitar chords hinted of the song to come.

'This is for Lucas Browne. Come on everyone, let's sing along with it now.'

I am just a poor boy.
Though my story's seldom told,
I have squandered my resistance
For a pocketful of mumbles,
Such are promises

Simon and Garfunkel's 'The Boxer', the very same song that was piped at lunch two weeks earlier in Grozny, the song that I associate with Lucas and the cruelty of his craft, was now being dedicated to him. Before we left that pub that night, many an Irishman or -woman told us that he or she had already known about Lucas and his unexpected but brave victory. Through Ricky Hatton's promotion, Lucas has a profile in Ireland and the United Kingdom, and we left Peadar Kearney's that Saint Patrick's Day night thinking that this was big and could get much bigger. Imagine a super fight with Tyson Fury, Anthony Joshua or David Haye. Now that would be something.

III. The News

The Clachaig Inn has stood alone like a stoic watchman guarding the surrounding landscape for over three hundred years, looking out upon the starkly beautiful glen that gives the Scottish village Glencoe its name. Deep in the Highlands, Glencoe nestles itself in among towering mountains, defying weather and treacherous history, both equally as grim. It was early spring in the northern hemisphere and mist had shrouded the burns and flowerless heather, while snow had capped the peaks that enclose the inn in their defiant majesty.

Climbers and adventure-seekers from around the world come to this inn. So too did two Australians revisiting the place of their family's origin, wanting to find some solitude and immerse themselves in the raw beauty of the untamed Highlands. It was Monday 21 March, four days after our uplifting experience in that Dublin pub and sixteen days since that intoxicating moment when Stanley Christodoulou stepped between the two fighters in Grozny. Matt and I planned to stay at this inn for three nights before driving south to the fertile farmlands of Lanarkshire, where our Clark clan still live and farm.

A munro is a mountain in Scotland that stands over three thousand feet – that's more than nine hundred metres. Many of the people that shared the Clachaig Inn with us did so with the intention of 'bagging' – scaling – a munro or two around Glencoe, maybe one of the imposing Three Sisters that guard the southern approach to the glen.

We, being Australian, wanted nothing more than to touch snow, but as it happened none lay lower than the lofty tops of the surrounding mountains. Common sense played no part in our decision-making; we took off for the lowest of these summits, dressed in tracksuit pants and trainers, three cough lozenges for food. Much later, with Scottish slush soaking our socks and an icy wind biting through our pathetically inadequate jumpers, we sat, holding snow, gazing out across the yawning glen, awestruck and humbled by the primeval, pristine glory before our eyes.

As silly as what we had just done was, yet another feeling of triumph settled upon us. Here, enveloped in the mystical Scottish Highlands, against all wisdom and good sense, we climbed a mountain and stood on its peak. Lucas Browne went to Grozny, Chechnya, to seek his Holy Grail and stood unconquered on its peak. Right there, on that munro in the Highlands, with snow in my hand and glorious Scotland before me, I believed I had tasted the elixir of life and it was indeed sweet. It was about to turn very sour.

While Matt and I traipsed through Ireland and Scotland, Lucas Browne had arrived back in Sydney to a triumphant welcome. His face was on national news broadcasts and the country's newspapers all carried major articles about his victory. He was on all the gig shows – breakfast TV shows, Channel Nine's *Footy Show*, Fox Sports' *The Back Page* and on radio chatting with Alan Jones. With his humble approach and ability to express himself eloquently, his profile was soaring. Book proposals and a film option rolled in. He must have felt that he had tasted the very same elixir of life.

Back in the Scottish Highlands, we ate dinner in a corner of the bar in the Clachaig Inn. With hikers and climbers deep in conversation, obedient dogs sitting at the feet of locals, and open log fires burning away, we talked with the couple nearby. The husband and wife were from Nottingham, England, and they visited the Highlands often, to soak up their beauty and isolation.

Cricket was our shared passion and, of course, English and Australian rivalry raised its head. I wanted to focus on English all-rounder Stuart Broad's refusal to walk after snicking one in the Ashes in 2013, coincidentally at Nottingham's Trent Bridge, and about Mitchell Johnson's destruction of the English batting line-up in the return series in Australia. Unsurprisingly, our companions wished to talk more about

Broad's decimation of the Aussies with the swinging ball on their home pitches. So we changed the subject.

As they were about to depart, the woman's conversation faltered, as if she was having second thoughts about what she was about to say. We let it pass and she and her husband stood to leave. He then turned towards us with tears welling in his eyes. His wife, who had so warmly opened up to us over the past hour, had inoperable cancer and had little time left to live. Moments like these, finding solace in the Scottish Highlands, must have been so precious to this couple, and they had shared a few of those minutes with us. There was very little to be said, but perhaps our embraces and whispered wishes said enough. Our paths had crossed for such a short time in the warmth of this Highland pub and then they departed, into the chill that lurked just outside the pub door. A chill was about to descend upon us.

We sat alone, lost in our own thoughts, lubricated by pints of Guinness. Matt's phone rang. And everything changed.

Philippe Fondu was sitting in his home in Belgium. With the froth of Guinness to my lips, I watched Matt's face and I could tell by his tone that the news was not good.

'Lucas has tested positive to clenbuterol.'

Clenbuterol? I had heard of clenbuterol, but right then I had no idea about what it did or what it was used for. In those thick, stony moments as we sat in silence, all I needed to know was that it was a banned substance and it was present in the A sample from Lucas's post-fight urine test.

All types of scenarios ran through my mind. Had Lucas inadvertently consumed it in a supplement? Could it be an inaccurate result; did testing agencies make errors like that?

Had something he ingested while in Grozny contained the substance?

There were many questions that could have been asked in those minutes, but words never came. Stunned and heavy silence descended upon us. The news had leaked out to the media, who knew about it before any of the management team, even before Browne himself. Matt picked up his phone and pressed Lucas's number. No answer. It was early morning back home, but this news couldn't wait. He tried again.

In the early morning light, Lucas Browne was woken by the incessant vibration of his phone on the bedside table. When he checked his phone, he noticed it wasn't just one caller, but multiple numbers on his missed call screen. He saw Matt's number. Guessing it must be important, Browne answered the call. Browne sat on the side of his bed, his phone to his ear, his life changing. He was bewildered, unable to grasp how it could be possible:

> I had been still asleep and I had my phone on silent.
> It had been going ballistic and I saw that Matt had
> been trying to ring me, so when I saw it was him again,
> I answered. Basically my heart just sank when he
> told me. I sat there and thought 'Wow, what is going
> on?' I didn't know which test it was, before or after
> the fight, I had no idea how or why. I was completely
> gutted. I knew I hadn't taken anything at all, not
> even a pre-workout supplement, which I knew other
> athletes had got inadvertently done for in the past. I was
> absolutely particular about everything I did and took
> into my body.

The news slammed home to the boxer, his loved ones, his team, and his supporters, as well as the wider Australian public, with the subtlety of one of his own right hands. As perplexing as the news was to Browne, one implication was unmissable: his victory in Grozny and therefore his status as the WBA regular heavyweight champion was in jeopardy. He had just been branded a drug cheat; it does not get any worse than that. In the days that followed, Browne's world was turned upside down. The media went from showering him in lavish praise to chasing an angle on a drug-cheating scandal. Much of corporate Australia that had been swooning over him now turned the other way. Browne was bewildered and angry, unable to explain the positive result to himself or to others.

IV. Some Form of Contamination

By the time he faced the press and declared his innocence, some encouraging news had filtered through to Lucas Browne's camp. The results for his pre-fight testing proved negative. There it was, as far as he and his team were concerned; he had arrived in Grozny clean of all banned substances. The clenbuterol that was in his system had been consumed in Grozny. Browne and Hatton Promotions released a statement detailing their stance. It read:

I would like to assure all of my fans, the whole of the boxing world and all of Australia that I am not a drug user or a drug cheat. The news of this positive test has shocked and devastated me. I will be fighting for as long as it takes to clear my name. Prior to today, I had not heard of the drug clenbuterol and had no idea of what it was used for. I am now aware that it is essentially a weight-stripping drug and as a heavyweight boxer the idea of me using it is utterly ridiculous. I am a staunch long-term opponent of any drug use, performance-enhancing or otherwise.

A short time later another press release was issued, detailing the negative results from the pre-fight testing, establishing Browne's status as a clean athlete upon his arrival in Grozny. The statement from Browne included his team's planned way forward:

My team's investigation will now concentrate on the period of time between the clean test on February 29th and the fight itself on March 5th. I maintain that I did not knowingly consume any banned substance, including the clenbuterol found in my system in that time.

Browne is an avid user of social media. At this critical point in his career, it became an uplifting avenue of support for him, but it was equally a haunt for the mudslingers. He was derided as a steroid user, even though clenbuterol is not a steroid. The confusion arose perhaps because the World Anti-Doping Agency (WADA) bans clenbuterol under a listing of anabolic agents (not anabolic steroids). 'Anabolic' refers to building tissue and storing energy. The more Browne learned about clenbuterol, the more absurd became the notion that he would knowingly consume the drug prior to his bout. Clenbuterol lies within a class of drugs known as Beta-2 agonists, sharing some effects with stimulant drugs. It has been found to dilate bronchial tubes (hence its use in inhalers for asthmatics), to stimulate the central nervous system, increase heart rate and, importantly, burn excess body fat and increase muscle bulk. Clenbuterol is a thermogenic drug – one that increases core body heat through metabolic stimulation. This temperature rise, when combined with dieting and exercise, burns off fat, hence its use by bodybuilders seeking a quick – illegal – way to sculpt their bodies for competition.

The drug comes in numerous forms: syrups, aerosols, tablets, gels and liquid drops. Its side effects can be seriously debilitating. A user may suffer sleeplessness, anxiousness, elevated blood pressure, insomnia, an irregular heartbeat and a narrowing of blood vessels.

It makes no sense for a heavyweight boxer to risk those symptoms – especially for no benefit. It's not as if Browne had to lose weight – there is no upper limit in the heavyweight division. And would his team risk drug-smuggling through Australian and Russian customs?

That left two possible scenarios: either a meal Browne consumed had been inadvertently contaminated with clenbuterol through livestock feed; or food that the fighter was served had been deliberately laced with the drug to bring about a failed drug test.

But WBA regulations are clear, and in accordance with those of most sporting organisations: the athlete is responsible for what goes into his or her system.

Clenbuterol has claimed some big names in sport. By far the biggest name undone by a positive test is the Spanish cyclist Alberto Contador.

Contador failed a test during the 2010 Tour de France, which he won – and lost, because of the drug test. The Spaniard was banned for two years, and was also stripped of a subsequent victory in the 2011 Giro d'Italia. On appeal, the Court of Arbitration for Sport found Contador had 'probably' ingested a food supplement contaminated with the banned substance, so small were the traces detected. But the ban and loss of his titles stayed in place.

Australian cyclist Michael Rogers had his reputation linked to clenbuterol in 2013, when he tested positive to small amounts of the drug. A gold medal winner at the 1998 Kuala Lumpur Commonwealth Games and a stage winner in the top-flight Grand Tour events, Rogers was exonerated of any fault by cycling's governing body, the International Cycling Union, which declared there was a high probability that the cyclist consumed contaminated meat while in China. His career was allowed to continue.

Sports such as swimming, American baseball, Mexican soccer, Australian Rules football and, of course, boxing have been tainted by association with clenbuterol. In many cases, the athlete has put up the same defence – the clenbuterol was in something they ate.

While most of the Western world has banned the use of clenbuterol in feedstock, other regions have not. It is fed to cattle, pigs and sheep to produce leaner meats in places such as China, Russia and Mexico. At soccer's FIFA under-17 World Cup in Mexico in 2011 more than 100 players tested positive to clenbuterol. FIFA then ordered testing of the food from their hotels – almost one-third of the food tested came back positive to the drug.

But the fact remained: Lucas Browne had somehow had ingested a banned substance while in Grozny.

Consequently, a letter, dated 22 March, was issued to Browne from the office of the law firm Smith Alling, based in Tacoma, in Washington State, USA. The letter established that the firm represented the World Boxing Association and that Browne had tested positive to clenbuterol in his A sample, taken on 5 March 2016 (in fact, it was the early hours of the following day when the sample was provided).

Browne was further advised that if he wished to contest the finding by having his B sample tested, he had until 28 March to inform the WBA of his intention. The letter concluded by stating that if there was to be no challenge, the WBA would issue a resolution on the matter in the following weeks.

The next day a response was issued from the law office of high-profile lawyer and boxing promoter Leon Margules. Margules had worked behind the scenes in bringing the Chagaev–Browne fight together and now was cast in the role of Lucas Browne's key legal representative.

His letter was addressed to the WBA president, Gilberto Mendoza, asserting that Browne did not knowingly take clenbuterol into his system prior to his fight. It informed that Browne's team had launched a thorough investigation and requested that the WBA do likewise. The background of past drug issues in Russia – and the unusual case of Fres Oquendo's positive test in Grozny – were cited as reasons to not treat this as an 'open and shut' case.

Importantly, Margules requested a response from the WBA, asking what procedures it had in place to initiate an inquiry into the circumstances surrounding Browne and also the procedures to request a full evidentiary hearing of his case.

Meanwhile, VADA president Margaret Goodman issued a notice dated 1 April stating that the testing of Browne's specimen from the time in Grozny was now complete. It verified what the team already knew: that, with the exception of the post-fight testing, all other samples had proven negative. The B sample from the night of the fight had not yet been tested, and the Browne legal team requested that it be tested too, though they did so expecting it too would test positive to the drug. Still awaiting a reply to his earlier letter, a concerned Leon Margules wrote to the body again, on 13 April, and was quite explicit in his request. He asked the WBA to take no action against his client until he was given due process and a full hearing on the matter. The lawyer informed the WBA that the process of proving Browne to be a clean athlete who did not voluntarily ingest the banned substance would take at least a few more weeks. It also reminded the association that, once action was taken against Browne, irreparable damage would be done to his career and his reputation, irrespective of whether the decision was later reversed.

Concurrently two important developments took place. Browne's team contracted an independent expert to analyse all the information from the drug-testing process. As further data, Browne supplied hair follicles for further testing, as traces of clenbuterol can be detected and accurately dated in hair long after they have passed through the digestive system.

Dr Daniel Eichner is the resident of the Sports Medicine Research and Testing Laboratory operating out of Salt Lake City in the US state of Utah and is highly regarded for his expertise in the field of sports anti-doping. He analysed the VADA results and tested Browne's hair follicles, which were forwarded from Australia in a sealed plastic bag. His conclusions were clear: he found that the data was consistent with Browne having ingested a single dose of clenbuterol, and not from having abused the drug on an ongoing basis. He also concluded that the substance must have been ingested after the Monday of fight week.

Secondly, on 15 April, Lucas Browne voluntarily undertook a polygraph test. The test passed his assertion that he did not knowingly consume any banned substance. While a lie detector test carries no weight in Australian courts, it was yet another hoop that Browne had willingly jumped through to prove his innocence. Browne's British promoter, Ricky Hatton, released a statement in support of the fighter the following day:

> We will keep going and do all that we can to prove his innocence. Matters are in the hands of the lawyers and the World Boxing Association. I and the whole of boxing hope they do the right thing by Lucas. Boxing needs that to happen to maintain its credibility.

V. Clouds of Intrigue

So, by late April, at least some aspects of this murky set of circumstances had crystallised. Browne, having defeated

Chagaev in the ring in Grozny, had, post-fight, tested positive to minute traces of the banned substance clenbuterol. The drug was ingested while in Chechnya, as he was tested negative by VADA on the Monday before the fight. Consequently, lawyers acting on behalf of the WBA informed Browne of their intention to make a resolution in regard to his status in the following weeks.

In response, the boxer's legal team requested an open process of inquiry into the circumstances surrounding Browne's failed test and the opportunity for evidence to be submitted in Browne's defence. They warned of the perils of acting without due process. Further, the WBA was requested to respond, detailing the procedures they would take in the matter.

The wider backdrop to the drama was that it all happened in Russia; Chechnya is a Russian state. Just as Browne's case was unfolding, investigations of a more far-reaching and disturbing nature were taking place. A 2015 report by WADA detailed suspicions of systemic doping practices in Russian sport, and now United States prosecutors had launched their own investigation into state-sponsored doping schemes in Russia. Dramatically, a former director of the Russian testing laboratory, Grigory Rodchenkov, alleged that he personally switched positive urine samples with clean ones during the Sochi Winter Olympics to protect Russian athletes – and that the Russian intelligence services had devised a way of tampering with urine samples, by breaking the seal and substituting clean urine. As a result, the Russian track and field team would be banned from competing at the 2016 Rio de Janeiro Olympic Games in August.

In Browne's case there was never a question about the validity of the result or the integrity of the agency that performed the testing. Simply, the murkiness of Russian sport at the time just added further weight to the argument that his was a case that needed to be treated carefully. Browne's legal team believed that an open and full inquiry into his case by the WBA would likely lead to his name being cleared. Precedent was on his side. Fres Oquendo had travelled to Grozny in July 2014 and had come away with a defeat at the hands of Ruslan Chagaev and a positive result to a banned substance – essentially a breast cancer drug. Just as illogical as a one-off clenbuterol reading, Oquendo's test result saw no adverse action taken against him by the governing body. In fact, the WBA mandated that the American was entitled to a rematch with the champion. In those weeks spent trying to clear his name, the case of Mexican Francisco Vargas emerged. Under a differing sanctioning body, the WBC super featherweight world champion tested positive to clenbuterol while in training for his title fight with Orlando Salido in June. That organisation, the World Boxing Council, exonerated Vargas and declared him a clean athlete. WBC president, Mauricio Sulaiman, ruled that livestock being contaminated by clenbuterol is an ongoing issue in Mexico and other regions of the world.

Would the WBA think along the same lines as the WBC? Would it act as it did in the case of Oquendo? On Thursday 12 May – appropriately Friday the thirteenth in Australia – the WBA delivered its resolution. The organisation ruled that Browne be stripped of his world title and banned from boxing for six months. It declared that his status in the rankings would be reconsidered at the conclusion of the ban. Further, Ruslan Chagaev was reinstated as the WBA regular world champion and was granted 120 days to negotiate a fight with the mandatory challenger, Fres Oquendo. The WBA restated their position that, in their view, it was entirely the responsibility of the boxer and his team to monitor what goes into his body and that there was no way for them to determine the validity of Browne's assertion that he had been contaminated.

Lucas Browne was devastated. The belt that he had won so courageously in the ring in Grozny had been stripped from him. It hurt all the more that he had never actually received a belt from the WBA. In effect, what he had achieved in his battle with Ruslan Chagaev was threatened to be wiped from the history books of boxing, the fight being declared a 'no contest', and no longer could he proudly wear the mantle of Australia's first ever world heavyweight champion. Browne's team believed implicitly in his innocence; they knew him as an anti-drug advocate, one who had never tested positive to any banned substance previously. And it was Browne's team who had insisted on a testing schedule conducted by VADA as one of the terms of the fight contract.

The positive result to clenbuterol and the subsequent action taken by the WBA had turned the boxer's fortunes upside down. He had plunged from the rarefied heights of sporting achievement, where the corporate world came wooing and even more lucrative fights were beckoning, down to the depths of sporting shame. His earning power had been devastated.

Browne's team examined his legal options and on 17 June a lawsuit was filed by Browne against the WBA in the

Superior Court in Tacoma in the state of Washington in the United States. It was submitted by the law firm Van Siclen, Stocks & Firkins, acting under instruction from attorney Leon Margules, and it sought an unspecified amount for the damage done to Browne's boxing career and his reputation. The legal action included a motion for preliminary injunction, the purpose of which was to restrain the WBA from imposing any consequences upon Browne as a result of his failed drug test. More precisely, it sought his restoration as world champion and the six-month suspension to be lifted. At its core, the suit contended that Browne had a legal right to have his interests restored through the court because he had been denied due process before the WBA imposed its sanctions on him; the WBA had provided him with no opportunity for a hearing or to provide any materials in his defence.

Browne was fighting yet another title battle but now, in this one, the punches would be points of law and the principle of natural justice.

As with every bout, there would be supporters in both camps. In one corner would be those who supported the WBA's policy-driven stance, believing that an athlete is totally responsible for whatever enters his system, irrespective of circumstances.

In the other would be those who believed that the ingestion was a result of food contamination in Chechnya – and further that the WBA, while it acted strictly according to policy with Browne, had applied a completely different approach and outcome for Oquendo. The battle lines had been drawn and the case was set down for hearing in the Superior Court of Washington State for 21 July. With legal proceedings pending, Browne and his support team bunkered down. Meanwhile the whirlwind of euphoria and goodwill that Browne's mighty win in Grozny had created had dissipated like a passing storm; there in all its awesome majesty one moment, swept away on some random tailwind the next.

Now it was almost as if the fight had never happened. The achievement had been wiped from the records, the glory had been tarnished and the story had been retold, the hero now cast as the villain.

But Browne's self-belief had not been shaken. He continued to keep in shape, constantly working in the gym and doing sparring sessions. He had kept his weight hovering around 115 kilograms, not much heavier than he recorded for the Chagaev bout. He was fit and focused. Sitting in a coffee shop in Perth just before the lawsuit was filed, he radiated self-confidence with a simple and direct strategy. 'If they have taken this world title away from me, then I'm just going to win another.'

On the timescale of the courts, the events of late July and August moved at breakneck speed. Legal teams met behind closed doors and the hearing set down for 21 July was adjourned until 4 August.

Then came more stunning news: Ruslan Chagaev was to be stripped of the world title belt that had been restored to him.

The WBA had issued a resolution seeking payment of sanction fees dating back to his 2014 bout with Fres Oquendo – the one that had resulted in his positive test – with 14 July 2016 the deadline. The date came and went without payment and the association moved on the boxer. On 22 July, Chagaev was removed from the WBA's rankings, his world title stripped from him and all recognition of him by the association withdrawn.

In the meantime, Browne got on the front foot and became Australia's first boxer to enlist in the WBC and VADA joint initiative, the Clean Boxing Program. In doing so, he made himself available for random drug testing at any time on any day of the year.

'I have absolutely no issues with this as I am a clean athlete and I believe boxing needs this kind of regulation,' he announced confidently. 'I welcome this aspect of safety for the sport of boxing. I despise all drugs, whether they be performance-enhancing or recreational.'

Shortly afterwards, Chagaev announced his retirement. Since his defeat in the ring in Grozny, the former champion had been out of the public eye and had not responded to the WBA's directive to engage in negotiations with Oquendo in defence of his reinstated title.

He cited deteriorating eyesight in his left eye as the reason for his decision. It was the eye that Browne's team had identified as a vulnerable target in the title showdown.

Boxing websites were by now awash with speculation about Chagaev's relinquished regular world title. Rumours started to circulate that Browne's next fight might be for that title, the one stripped from him. The two names that were most mentioned were Fres Oquendo and the Englishman David Haye. But at that stage, it was all just guesswork and talk, with Browne still serving out his six-month suspension.

However, Lucas Browne's lawsuit against the WBA was withdrawn on 4 August, as the two legal teams had reached an out-of-court agreement. And what an agreement it was.

VI. Redemption Song

He stood alone on Monument Hill, Perth, lost in thought, anonymous in the pre-dawn darkness. He breathed in the chill September morning air, allowing himself to feel satisfied, vindicated even. Lucas Browne was back in the game.

In this place dedicated to the fallen soldiers of World War I, he stood on high ground, dressed in tracksuit pants and a hoodie, staring out towards the east as the approaching dawn announced itself in a faint splash of lightening colour on the far horizon. His mind drifted back to Grozny, back to that night, flashes of previously forgotten memories re-emerging and darting through his consciousness. He recalled standing among the Chechen crowd on the viewing platform at the Colosseum Sports Hall, watching a preliminary fight, getting a feel for the atmosphere. As he leaned forward, his hands resting on the rail in front, he looked more at the ring than the fight inside it, that stretch of canvas that would be his gladiatorial arena. What he remembered above all else was the hand on his shoulder.

Directly behind him was Danny, his left hand upon his younger brother's right shoulder. The feel of that hand said everything that needed to be said: 'We are with you all the way, brother.' That hand on his shoulder had been a touchstone for all of the unwavering support during the troubles that followed.

His mind made abstract connections, throwing up snatches of forgotten moments. He thought of watching a TV monitor in the Colosseum gym as it showed Ali Funeka getting into the ring, and he remembered the track that accompanied him, Bob Marley's 'Redemption Song'. Browne wanted redemption himself.

The eastern sky was now awash with pastel blue and orange. Lucas Browne had nowhere he had to be, no pressing engagement, no demands. Well, not for a few hours anyway. For the moment, everything was calm. His suspension was over. For him, something new had just begun.

As he stood on Monument Hill, he took heart from the guarantee that his next bout would again be for the heavyweight title of the world.

Equally he knew that the negotiations could be protracted and the where and when of the bout were far from certain. Those details were not critical issues for him at that moment. What mattered most was that he would have the opportunity to put right the wrong done to him. Just the week before he had flown with manager Matt Clark to the United States to meet with his lawyer, Leon Margules. There he had signed off on the settlement that had been agreed upon between his camp and the WBA, allowing the organisation's Championship Committee to issue a resolution regarding his status. The contents of that resolution now ran through his thoughts.

The single word that his mind kept coming back to was 'exceptional'. That was the word that the WBA used to describe the circumstances that led to a revision of their original decision. He agreed wholeheartedly with their description.

In setting the background to their decision, the WBA listed a number of central issues that swirled around his case. The WBA cited the negative result from Browne's pre-fight test.

The WBA acknowledged that the previous fight in Grozny – between Chagaev and Oquendo – had also culminated in an accusation of poisoning. It pointed out that

WADA had suspended Russia's anti-doping laboratory and agency for failing to follow proper procedures.

To sum up the 'exceptional' circumstances, the WBA acknowledged that Browne had arrived in a country where the use of performance-enhancing drugs was 'rampant' and where there was a history of 'poisoning' competitors – and that Browne had arrived a clean athlete.

Further, the WBA resolution recognised the illogicality of Browne ingesting a banned drug with zero potential benefit. They concluded:

> It is highly unlikely Browne intentionally or voluntarily ingested clenbuterol in a single small dose in the days leading up to the bout as the amount would not have gained any advantage – especially in the heavyweight division.

All precisely as the boxer had been protesting from the start.

The WBA also noted Browne's willingness to undergo future random drug testing and his 'acknowledgement that the WBA Rules and procedures shall govern all future matters and disputes'. Critically, the resolution stated that the Australian's suspension was 'the minimum available under the WBA Rules, but mandatory, due to the WBA's strict policy regarding a positive prohibited-substance test'. Now, the six months were up. He could fight again.

The resolution rang through Lucas Browne's mind like the chiming of church bells – or maybe AC/DC's bells. The statue of their original frontman, Bon Scott, was just nearby, his grave just down the road. The WBA had made three crucial rulings. Browne's ranking would be in the top five of the WBA. More importantly, within 120 days of his suspension ending on 5 September, he would fight Fres Oquendo for the WBA world heayweight title. And if for any reason Oquendo was not available, Browne would fight the leading available contender for the vacant title.

At the time the resolution was issued the WBA had Tyson Fury as the Super Champion of the World. From there its rankings were, from the top, Luis Ortiz, Wladimir Klitschko, Alexander Ustinov, Fres Oquendo and David Haye. Now Lucas 'Big Daddy' Browne would re-enter that exclusive grading and fight for the regular world title.

He turned away from the dawning sky. He was ready for all that lay ahead.

VII. Tearing Up His Ticket

Hours later, at just before ten in the morning, the fighter took his place in front of microphones, cameras and journalists. Unlike many of his recent press conferences, this one was characterised by smiles and light-hearted banter, the mood reflecting the upturn in Browne's fortunes. After gathering his thoughts that early morning on Monument Hill, he answered questions with the clarity and certainty of a man in control of his life.

His frustration and anger at what had transpired were barely disguised. While acknowledging the complexities of the WBA's position following his positive test result, for the first time in six months he was able to reveal his quietly bubbling anger. 'To be perfectly honest, I'm slightly pissed off. I technically had the belt for about a week before it all came crashing down. So I'm having to start from scratch,' Browne explained.

But there was no mistaking which emotion dominated his thinking that morning: it was a determination born of a sense of being wronged.

'I really want to do some damage to the next person and come out and show everyone that I am the world champion,' the fighter snarled.

Later that day, speaking to presenter Adam Shand on Perth radio 6PR, he was even more specific in referring to his next opponent. 'If Fres wants to step up to the plate, I hope to retire him also,' he said, in regard to Ruslan Chagaev's recent retirement.

And then, just in case any fan or listener was still unclear about Lucas Browne's thoughts about the past six months, he allowed himself to look backwards one last time. Yes, it had all happened to him once in Grozny, he had journeyed there among the Chechen people and challenged their hero, Ruslan Chagaev. In the fire of combat, he had triumphed. For the rest of his life, Grozny should have been his crowning glory. Instead it would forever be the place where he was never going to win, no matter what he did in the ring.

'I don't want to set foot in Chechnya ever again,' he said. Nothing more needed to be said.

The negotiations for Browne's fight for redemption stretched from September into mid October and the only thing out in the public arena was speculation. Behind the scenes though, doors were shutting and far more lucrative ones were opening.

The WBA heavyweight landscape changed dramatically during those weeks. Browne's mandated opponent, Fres Oquendo, informed the WBA that he was unable to meet any fight commitments due to a lingering shoulder injury. So with Oquendo out of the reckoning, Browne's team looked elsewhere.

Then a seismic shock rocked the boxing world. At the beginning of October, the WBA super heavyweight champion Tyson Fury announced on social media his retirement from boxing, aged just 27. Within hours he rescinded his decision. Then he changed his mind again. Concurrently he gave a warts-and-all interview that sounded like a cry for help, as he admitted to self-medicating his mental problems with cocaine. Those problems were on display in the *Rolling Stone* interview, in which he said he wanted someone to kill him, to release him from the torment of his depression. In the background, Fury was under investigation at the time by the United Kingdom Anti-Doping Agency.

Fury had taken the WBA, WBO, WBC and IBF heavyweight titles when he had beaten Wladimir Klitschko in November 2015. Their rematch was off once Fury quit the sport. That left Klitschko free, and the Browne team went chasing him.

Very few fight fans were aware just how close the Browne team came to stitching up a deal with Klitschko's camp for a 10 December showdown in Hamburg. Behind-the-scenes negotiations had been underway for some time before the boxing public started to hear rumours that the reinstated

Australian just might fall on his feet, securing a comeback bout with the biggest name in heavyweight boxing. Negotiators representing the Ukrainian sounded out Browne's representatives on more than one occasion, each time with an improved set of terms. The offer to Browne stood at just over US$1 million. Klitschko no doubt saw Browne as an opponent with credibility, but one who he believed he would defeat. Browne saw Klitschko as the opportunity of a lifetime.

As the two teams got closer to a deal, the Klitschko handlers suddenly withdrew and commenced discussion with IBF world champion Anthony Joshua, for what would be a fight for the title of super champion – but only if the WBA was willing to sanction the bout. Klitschko was intent on winning back his coveted WBA super title. Browne was now without a fight, but with a number of credible options swirling around him.

Then, in late October, the WBA stepped in and cleared the waters. Klitschko would fight the undefeated Joshua for the super championship while Browne was to contest the regular title against the highly eccentric trash-talking American Shannon Briggs. The fight was to take place before the end of the year, with the winner to defend his title against Fres Oquendo within four months.

The waters didn't stay clear for long; Klitschko injured his shoulder in a training mishap and pulled out of his commitment with the Briton. But for Browne, the way ahead was unchanged: beat Briggs and he was WBA regular heavyweight champion. His destiny was in his own hands.

He went into intense training in Sydney with trusted mentor Rodney Williams. Back in familiar surroundings at the Blacktown PCYC, the boxer fell quickly into routine, Williams firm about his expectations and explicit in his aims. Foot movement, evasion, combinations and fitness; his mantra again all about muscle memory and self-discipline.

On the other side of the world, boxing lawyer Leon Margules had commenced discussions with the Briggs camp to reach an agreement and bring the two fighters together. Most boxers pay little notice to the countless hours of work that backroom support staff put in. The time spent on phones, in front of laptops, in meetings and in gyms, researching, planning, negotiating, arguing a case, selling a point of view and delivering an outcome largely pass by without acknowledgement.

Together with Philippe Fondu, Margules had worked overtime securing Browne his initial opportunity against Chagaev, a title shot for a boxer who had yet to meet an opponent ranked in the top 15 in his division. He then led the complex and sophisticated legal challenge to clear the boxer's name and have him reinstated to the highest ranks of heavyweight boxing. Now here he was again, doing what he does so very well: negotiating to provide his man with the most favourable deal that he could.

Then in late November, with another world title fight fast approaching, an email brought everything crashing down.

Manager Matt Clark received the email, from VADA president Margaret Goodman. It informed him that random testing conducted on Tuesday 8 November on Lucas Browne under the WBC Clean Boxing Program had resulted in an adverse finding for the banned substance ostarine. Clark forwarded the email on to Philippe Fondu, Leon Margules and to the boxer himself.

Abject despair, stunned impotence and no small degree of anger descended upon the whole team.

As with the previous positive result to clenbuterol, Browne was unable to explain the finding. This time, sabotage or eating contaminated foods could be immediately dismissed. All notions of a wronged fighter seeking redemption had been blown away.

Browne's manager summed up the feelings of the entire team. 'It's like he won Lotto and someone tore up his winning ticket. And then he won it a second time, and it got torn up again.'

VIII. Rocky Marciano Didn't Need Them

Some high-profile figures in international boxing had fought tirelessly to win back what had been taken from Browne in Chechnya, but now it seemed their only reward would be sullied reputations and a sense of betrayal.

But in the maelstrom of emotion that descended upon the team, once they shook off the initial shock and bewilderment, they went back to work.

Philippe Fondu's experience and contact book now became vital as he gathered the energy to yet again mount an investigation into how this positive result could have happened. Leon Margules now had the difficult task of continuing discussion with the Briggs camp, hamstrung by this debilitating development. However, the alternative made little sense: there was nothing to be gained by sitting back and waiting for a WBA ruling. And Matt Clark's job was clear: to determine how ostarine had entered Browne's body.

The list of prohibited substances is very detailed and ostarine is found under the heading 'Other Anabolic Agents'. Categorised under a class of substances known as SARMs – selective androgen receptor modulators – ostarine, like clenbuterol, is not a steroid, but has some similar effects on the body to steroids. It was developed for the treatment of conditions such as muscle atrophy and is known to repair muscle damage, promote joint healing and improve endurance.

Also known as enobosarm and MK-2866, ostarine, unlike clenbuterol, is something that would help a boxer. Its promoters say that it can help a boxer bulk up with lean, non-fatty muscle, which increases strength. They claim that it promotes muscle growth just like steroids, but without the side effects. No bad breath, no acne, no aggro, no man boobs (steroids promote oestrogen production). The 'selective' part in SARM is what reduces the side effects. Ostarine also allegedly helps in retaining nitrogen, which itself helps to strengthen the body. Unlike steroids, it is said to be non-toxic to the liver – and it's taken orally, so no needles. The sales pitch is seductive, and ostarine has found no shortage of fans among gym rats, especially bodybuilders. That, despite the fact it has never been legalised, never approved for human consumption. The only way to buy it is for the seller to market it for 'research purposes'. Its long-term effect is entirely unknown.

A Tennessee company called GTx was testing ostarine as long as a decade ago, and applied unsuccessfully to have it licensed in the US as a drug to treat muscle wastage. In 2016 the US Food and Drug Administration agency was investigating whether ostarine was being used in dietary supplements – typically protein supplements taken by bodybuilders. GTx has issued notices to several supplement manufacturers to stop using ostarine in their products.

What Browne revealed to Clark was that he had recently switched the supplement product that he was taking in workout recovery. This product had not been prescribed or vetted by a sports physician; its use had flown under the radar of his trainer and the boxer had accepted the supplier's word that it contained nothing untoward.

This development sent a secondary wave of disappointment and bewilderment through his management team. Here was their boxer, deep in training, with a world title tilt a matter of weeks away and subject to random testing anywhere at any time – and he uses a supplement without due diligence. As a boxing fan and friend forlornly put it: 'Why do they take those supplements? Rocky Marciano didn't need them. He was plenty tough enough just drinking water.' Lucas Browne saw it differently. He was an athlete in the twenty-first century where supplement use was commonplace, part of the regular intake of professional sportsmen and -women:

> In regard to the supps, I thought I was being very
> careful and doing the right thing. I'm not a cheat and
> have never wanted to be labelled that in any way. But
> I'm thirty-seven years old. I'm in a position to really
> make my dreams come true and I wanted to be able
> to give myself every chance to succeed by looking
> after myself, taking supplements after workouts and
> eating properly.

On 27 November WBC president, Mauricio Sulaiman, issued a warning to all boxers enrolled in his organisation's Clean Boxing Program, urging them to be careful in supplement usage. Issued under the program's slogan 'You use, you lose', in the warning Sulaiman acknowledged that many boxers were unknowingly consuming banned substances.

'There are very few intentional cases of doping,' he said. 'But some fighters simply don't know what's in the supplement they're swallowing.' As a case in point, he provided the example of the bantamweight fighter Edgar 'Power' Jimenez who, when asked if he was taking any supplements, confirmed that he was, but had no idea what they contained, only that a doctor had approved it for him.

Browne was not the first boxer to test positive to this anabolic agent. The former IBF super middleweight champion of the world, Lucian Bute, tested positive to ostarine post-fight in his showdown with the WBC title holder, Badou Jack, in Washington DC in April 2016. Jack retained his title after the drawn result, but Bute went away protesting that the substance had been present in a supplement he used. The fighter was subsequently fined $50,000, but suffered no further sanction.

In the wider world of fighting sports, the high-profile UFC fighter Tim Means also showed a positive result to ostarine. When he provided a sealed container of the supplement he was using, USADA found it did contain ostarine, which was not listed on the packaging. Means copped a six-month ban. The heavyweight boxer Bermane Stiverne also claims to have been caught in the VADA net due to supplement use. He tested positive to the prohibited drug dimethylamylamine, a dietary supplement connected to the treatment of ADHD and weight loss and also associated with enhanced bodybuilding outcomes. His team identified the post-workout supplement Superharm as containing the substance.

Stiverne had been locked into a world title elimination fight with Alexander Povetkin who, earlier that year, had his own dramas, when VADA testing revealed levels of the super energy agent meldonium, the drug associated with his Russian compatriot Maria Sharapova.

The WBC responded by fining Stiverne $75,000 – and permitting his fight against Povetkin to proceed on December 17.

Other boxers haven't been so fortunate. British heavyweight Dillian Whyte was banned for two years for ingesting a stimulant contained in the workout supplement Jack3D. On appeal a tribunal accepted that Whyte unknowingly consumed the banned substance but ruled that he lacked discernment and diligence in monitoring the supplement's additives.

Fellow Brit Abdul-Bari Awad – known better by his nickname 'Kid Galahad' – similarly copped a two-year ban for detection of the steroid stanozolol, which he claimed was in a protein shake spiked by his brother.

The WBC world super featherweight champion Francisco Vargas and a pair of former world title holders, Tyson Fury and Antonio Tarver, have all suffered adverse test results and, in the world of UFC, fighters such as Hector Lombard, Brock Lesnar, Lyoto Machida and Anderson Silva have faced sanctions for their actions.

Now Lucas Browne found himself back among this chaos, so shortly after he had been thrown a safety line. This time his immediate future looked bleak, his only hope lying in his team identifying the origins of the ostarine in his body. And then, of course, hoping that the WBA would see fit to fine him a portion of his prize money, but allow his career to continue.

If his team was able to detect ostarine by testing his supplements, they would then have some line of argument that the product was inaccurately labelled, thereby contributing significantly to Browne's predicament. That was now where their efforts were concentrated.

IX. Downfall of a Hero

It was late on a steamy Sydney evening in February 2016 and Lucas Browne was sitting at his laptop. In a few days' time he would fly to Grozny for his world title bout. Very few pundits gave him a chance; after all, he had yet to even face a top-ranked opponent. Maybe the finishing touch on his preparation just might be a small dose of self-belief; another's triumph of spirit and willpower can light a fire in our souls.

Years earlier, a young Browne had a hero, an antihero in the eyes of many, the 'baddest man on the planet', Mike Tyson. Browne's pet dog was named Tyson. The fury that 'Iron' Mike unleashed in the ring left quite an impression on the boy Browne. Tyson was indestructible; he swept aside challengers with disdain; he was a primeval, malicious force that was seemingly impregnable to attack – until he met James 'Buster' Douglas. As a boy Browne had watched the downfall of his hero, scarcely believing it. And now, more than a quarter of a century later, he was about to watch that fight again. When James 'Buster' Douglas stepped into the Tokyo Dome ring that 11 February 1990, he had already been defeated four times in his career and bookmakers assessed his odds of upsetting the champion at around 40–1. Tyson held the WBA, WBC, IBF and lineal titles, making him the undefeated, undisputed champion of the world. He had knocked out thirty-two of his previous thirty-seven opponents. They weren't journeymen; his victims included Trevor Berbick, Larry Holmes, Michael Spinks and Frank Bruno. On top of that was his aura in the ring: seething, vicious and vengeful.

So the bell rang and the greatest upset in heavyweight boxing was underway. The first round laid the platform for the rest of the fight. Initially Douglas appeared a little jumpy and gun-shy when Tyson circled him menacingly, but as the round progressed he was looking sharper and more agile than the champion, whose preparation had been poor. As the first round drew to a close Douglas landed a jolting right cross on Tyson's chin and the challenger would have gone to his corner with his self-belief intact.

As Browne watched the next few rounds he saw Douglas's snapping jab accumulate points and his skill in tying Tyson up when he got into his familiar killing grounds. Exchanges were heavy at times, but each time Douglas was coming away on top. The further the fight went on, the more frustrated and off his game Tyson appeared to be. Most spectators expected that the champion just had to weather the storm and take his chance later in the fight when it inevitably came. But, in the meantime, Douglas's superior boxing exhibition was taking a toll.

The challenger's straight right had been finding its mark and, for one of the first times in his career, Tyson was looking damaged, a mortal for all the world to see. Douglas must have been growing in confidence as he kept his opponent out with his jab and thwarted his biggest weapons by outwrestling him in close. And he was now landing some heavier combinations, including a vicious right cross followed by an equally thumping straight left on his opponent's chin in the fifth.

And if he or his corner noted the confusion across the ring at the end of that fifth round, they would have been further buoyed. The heavyweight champion's team had neglected to bring an Enswell to the fight. This indispensable piece of equipment is applied to a fighter's facial injuries to limit swelling. Maybe it was a sign of arrogance or maybe it was a simple error, but Tyson's corner was forced to fill a rubber glove with iced water and apply it to his puffy left eye. The fight was by now heavily in the underdog's favour. He was throwing more punches, landing more punches and scoring more points.

The skirmishes had been heavy at times, but the intensity of the fight was about to be ratcheted up even further.

In the eighth round, Douglas landed some telling right crosses to Tyson's head and forced the champion onto the ropes with only seconds to go. Tyson had been bullied and bashed and now had nowhere to go but forward. He loaded up his favourite weapon, his right uppercut, jumped towards Douglas and unleashed it. It found its mark. Douglas slumped to the canvas. Referee Octavio Meyran bent to his knee beside the stricken fighter and commenced his count. The length of that count is part of boxing folklore, many claiming that its tardiness permitted Douglas to scramble to his feet in time. But regain his feet he did and the bell denied Tyson an opportunity to finish his assault.

Tyson came at Douglas early in the ninth, intent on finishing the fight. But Douglas fought him off and then launched his own salvos. The challenger forced the undefeated champion back against the ropes and then let loose with a battery of roundhouse lefts and rights that had Tyson staggering. Douglas's counterattack had not only fought off Tyson but returned the fight to his hands. The challenger was scoring with his jab in the tenth and final round. Tyson's eye had swelled and the accumulated damage caused by his opponent's radar-like punching was taking its toll. Tyson was wilting and his slowing evasive skills left him a tempting target for Douglas's bigger shots. One of them found home halfway through that tenth round.

Douglas cocked his right arm for an uppercut when he saw Tyson ducking to avoid his left jab and he let fly. The punch was sweet: Tyson reeled backwards. Douglas was on him in a flash and dispatched a left, right, left combination, all landing flush. The final left was a wicked blow to Tyson's jaw and the once invincible champion collapsed to the canvas.

As the count progressed, Tyson tried to stand, grabbing at his mouthguard. In his daze he placed it back in his mouth side on, with half protruding out of his mouth. The referee hugged the stricken boxer in close to signal the fight over and the most unexpected result in heavyweight history was complete.

Lucas Browne leaned back in his seat, hands clasped together behind his head, eyes still fixed on the computer screen, but his mind far away, dreaming of possibilities.

X. Rising Above or Sinking Below

That was ten months ago, and now, in December, much had changed. Lucas Browne had gone to Grozny and, like Buster Douglas, had taken on a world champion. Like Douglas he had dared to believe. Like Douglas, he had hit the canvas in the fight. Like Douglas, he got back up and immediately counterattacked. Like Douglas twenty-six years before him, he finished off the fight with a big right hand followed by a flurry of blows. Like Douglas, he achieved his dream.

As it turned out, in the events that were to follow, Browne may have gained more inspiration from Tyson's story than that of Douglas.

The fight to clear his name from the positive post-fight test for clenbuterol had been an exhausting one, a battle waged by management, lawyers and the boxer himself. They had been successful. The WBA reinstated him to the highest ranks of its heavyweights and ordered him to fight to regain the title stripped from him. Just when his chance at redemption was within range, dates and venue firming for his winnable title fight with Shannon Briggs, Browne's professional fortunes nosedived. A random test found ostarine in his system and, again, he was subject to public scrutiny as a drug cheat, this time through less-than-diligent scanning of the supplements he sourced.

The sporting public hardens its heart very quickly to a man who fumbles his second chance. Browne's promoter, Ricky Hatton, pointed out that the ostarine reading should count as a first offence, the WBA having in effect cleared the fighter of any wrongdoing in regard to the adverse result in Grozny. Hatton reminded critics that the fighter had voluntarily enrolled in the WBC Clean Boxing Program, subjecting himself to random testing, anytime, anywhere, 365 days a year. But mud sticks and the court of public opinion judges harshly.

No chemical analysis of his supplement was yet forthcoming and the World Boxing Association refrained from making any public comment concerning Browne's status until due process was observed. Browne had considered all the possibilities – a fine, a ban, the bout going ahead, the bout not going ahead. He had a lot to consider. But he had not given up hope. He still hungered for that world title belt:

> I'm just as disappointed about this test as I am about the first. I was and still am looking forward to making a statement on Briggs and kickstart the world title charge again. I think Briggs is a fight I need and still want. It's now a waiting game.

Browne thought of his boyhood hero, Mike Tyson, and his spiralling freefall from the dizzying heights of greatness to the ignominy of being jailed for rape. Other criminal charges dogged his life after his release. Browne had committed no crime or broken any laws of the land; he had consumed a supplement containing a banned substance.

In the days immediately following the VADA notification, he went through his own emotional tsunami, struggling to accept the hand that fortune was dealing him. He cryptically posted a message online: 'You can't defeat the demons you enjoy playing with.' He also shot some crude profanities at his detractors.

As for his 'demons', Lucas Browne has fears and insecurities like everyone. Like everyone, they shape who he is and what he does. But unlike most, the boxer is willing to reveal what drives him and what haunts him:

> My demons are in some ways normal and in other ways
> very dark. I have normal ones where you feel not good
> enough, or you worry about how you look. And then I
> have others where I have to control the violence in me.
> I think some of my demons are needed in regards to
> always keeping myself in check and always expecting
> better of myself. The darker ones relate to me and who
> I am, who I've always been and always kept under lock
> and key, away from people who don't know me. I know
> a violent urge is not looked upon as a good trait to have.
> But at the end of the day it is me and I feel I wouldn't be
> the boxer I am without it.

It is often our imperfections, our frailties and our limitations that create the conditions for any greatness we may harbour. When we are on our knees in life, we have really only two options: rising above and becoming more than we were, or sinking. The true greatness in all of us lies in our spirit, our willpower and our willingness to fight. Boxing exemplifies those traits, which is why it occupies the place in our society – in our collective consciousness – that it does. It is a theatre of drama and glory, challenge and tragedy; brutal and confronting at times, sublimely skilful at others. But sooner or later, just as in life, adversity catches up with every boxer who steps into the ring.

The power to overcome that lies in all of us is to do with our spirit, our willpower and our fight against the odds. Boxing has always enjoyed its place within the psyche of so many because, when all else is stripped away, it is all about spirit, willpower and the battle.

It is in how we respond to adversity that we define ourselves. Lucas Browne had that opportunity when he lay prone on his back in Grozny in the sixth round, Ruslan Chagaev looming over him, awaiting the chance to finish him off. Instead, the Australian refused to wilt and defined himself as a courageous and tenacious fighter.

Deep in an alien land, Lucas 'Big Daddy' Browne had stood on the foundations of a roadside billboard surrounded by young Chechen boys, each of them chanting his name. He had forged a bond of friendship with his gentle and intellectual Chechen translator, Adam Saidov, a survivor of war. It is a bond that now stretches across continents.

He had shared a boxing ring with a legend of the sport, the incomparable, dignified referee, Stanley Christodoulou. To this day, members of the Browne team keep in regular contact with Stan, swapping stories and paying respect.

He had spent time with a hardline president, one who had unexpectedly struck him with a punch to the midriff. He had rubbed shoulders as a fellow champion with Kostya Tszyu, a legend of the ring. He had walked the back alleyways of Grozny, mingling with those proud, unconquered people.

Along the way, former world heavyweight champions had sat up and taken notice; Johnny Lewis, the soul of Australian boxing, had nodded his admiration to the fighter. And he had stood in the middle of a boxing ring in Grozny, his arms raised in triumph, the mighty Ruslan Chagaev slumped in Stan Christodoulou's encircling arms, in that moment becoming the WBA heavyweight champion of the world.

Now, with all that had transpired, he knew that he may well have become the world champion who never was.

Rising above it all or sinking below it all – that was the simple choice that Lucas Browne now faced.

The boxer looked towards the future and made up his mind.

Author's Note

Deep inside me campfires blaze, their flickering flames penetrating the wilderness of my soul. Their glow brings enlightenment and wisdom where otherwise there would be ignorance and chaos. The power of this light is the belief that it nurtures, the belief that life can rise above the banal, that inside everyone is the potential for greatness, that we can all overcome the adversities that life throws at us.

Gathered around these fires are the keepers of the flame, those who have stoked the blazes and kept them burning throughout my life. During the writing of this book, one keeper of the flame passed away. He was 'The Greatest'. Muhammad Ali.

Without Ali, I might never have even started writing this book, for I would never have loved boxing in quite the way that I do. As a young boy, I fell in love with the theatre of Clay and Ali more than the sport itself. I recall so clearly the image of the fresh-faced Ali standing over the stricken Sonny

Liston and hearing the boast 'I am the greatest' uttered so confidently that I have believed it for a lifetime.

That his greatness then transcended the boxing ring cemented him in my psyche as a hero. His indomitable spirit, his conviction in his faith and his stand for social justice made him the most recognised man on Earth in the 1970s and beyond. The humour and drama that his fights were wrapped in elevated them to historical events rather than mere sporting contests. He inspired generations with the way he lived his life. Parkinson's disease could not conquer his dignity.

My favourite Ali quote should probably be 'The man with no imagination has no wings', but the fight fan in me wins out over the writer, so I favour this one: 'It's just a job. Grass grows, birds fly, waves pound the sand. I beat people up.'

With the passing of Muhammad Ali, one of the campfires of my soul was doused and, where there was once a light burning ever so brightly, for now, there is darkness. It will glow again, such was the power of this man.

'*Siylah* Muhammad Ali.'

Acknowledgements

Going to Grozny as a member of Team 'Big Daddy' for a world heavyweight title fight was the adventure of a lifetime for me. To have written *The World Champion That Never Was* and have it published is a dream come true. For all of that, I am indebted to a number of people.

My publisher, Pam Brewster, believed in the story from the outset and never gave up on it. I will be forever grateful.

My editor, Michael Epis, guided, advised and encouraged me throughout. Thanks, Mick, and all the staff who are part of the team at Hardie Grant.

To those legends of the boxing world, Johnny Lewis, Stanley Christodoulou and Kostya Tszyu, who all contributed so graciously to my book, and to those expert media personalities, Ben Damon and Steve Lillis, who did likewise; thank you so much. And I am most grateful to Philippe Fondu, Leonie Browne and the Browne family for entrusting their stories to me.

To my mates Dan, Dave, Matt and Des, all of who gave me constructive feedback and direction, I couldn't have done it without you.

To my fellow team members, who shared this extraordinary experience, particularly my son Matt, who makes me so proud through his love of boxing, but more so through the person he is. Thank you to all of you.

To my wife, Belinda, and my family, this would never have happened without your optimism and your blessing to 'go for it'. I hope you are proud.

Finally, to the boxer himself, Lucas 'Big Daddy' Browne, for it is he who risks it all in the ring. Without Lucas, without his courage, his tenacious spirit and without his dream to be a world champion, none of this would have happened. Thanks for the wild ride, mate, for the highs and the lows. I believe it's far from over yet.